RITE OF PENANCE

THE ROMAN RITUAL

Revised by Decree of the Second Vatican Ecumenical Council
and Published by Authority of Pope Paul VI

THE
RITE OF PENANCE

APPROVED FOR USE IN THE DIOCESES OF THE
UNITED STATES OF AMERICA BY THE
UNITED STATES CONFERENCE OF CATHOLIC BISHOPS
AND CONFIRMED BY THE APOSTOLIC SEE

With Complete Biblical Readings
Taken from the Revised Lectionary for Mass

English translation prepared by the
International Commission on English in the Liturgy

C.B.   P.C.

CATHOLIC BOOK PUBLISHING CORP.

NEW JERSEY

Concordat cum originali:

✠ Most Reverend Arthur J. Serratelli
   Chair of the USCCB Committee on Divine Worship
   in consultation with Monsignor Anthony F. Sherman
   Executive Director, USCCB Secretariat of Divine Worship

Permission to reprint this ritual with the revised selection of readings was given by the Congregation for Divine Worship and the Discipline of the Sacraments in a letter dated June 27, 2009 (Prot. No. 53.08/L).

Published by authority of the Bishops' Committee on Divine Worship, United States Conference of Catholic Bishops.

(T-528)

CONTENTS

SACRED CONGREGATION FOR DIVINE WORSHIP

Prot. n. 800/73

DECREE

Reconciliation between God and men was brought about by our Lord Jesus Christ in the mystery of his death and resurrection (see Romans 5:10). The Lord entrusted the ministry of reconciliation to the Church in the person of the apostles (see 2 Corinthians 5:18ff). The Church carries this ministry out by bringing the good news of salvation to men and by baptizing them in water and the Holy Spirit (see Matthew 28:19).

Because of human weakness, Christians "turn aside from [their] early love" (see Revelation 2:4) and even break off their friendship with God by sinning. The Lord, therefore, instituted a special sacrament of penance for the pardon of sins committed after baptism (see John 20:21-23), and the Church has faithfully celebrated the sacrament throughout the centuries—in varying ways, but retaining its essential elements.

The Second Vatican Council decreed that "the rite and formulas of penance are to be revised in such a way that they may more clearly express the nature and effects of this sacrament."[1] In view of this the Congregation for Divine Worship has carefully prepared the new **Rite of Penance** so that the celebration of the sacrament may be more fully understood by the faithful.

In this new rite, besides the **Rite for Reconciliation of Individual Penitents,** a **Rite for Reconciliation of Several Penitents** has been drawn up to emphasize the relation of the sacrament to the

---

[1] Second Vatican Council, constitution *Sacrosanctum Concilium,* no. 72: *AAS* 56 (1964) 118.

community. This rite places individual confession and absolution in the context of a celebration of the word of God. Furthermore for special occasions a **Rite for Reconciliation of Several Penitents with General Confession and Absolution** has been composed in accordance with the Pastoral Norms on General Sacramental Absolution, issue by the Congregation for the Doctrine of the Faith on June 16, 1972.[2]

The Church is solicitous in calling the faithful to continual conversion and renewal. It desires that the baptized who have sinned should acknowledge their sins against God and their neighbor and have heartfelt repentance for them, and it tries to prepare them to celebrate the sacrament of penance. For this reason the Church urges the faithful to attend penitential celebrations from time to time. This Congregation has therefore made regulations for such celebrations and has proposed examples or specimens which episcopal conferences may adapt to the needs of their own regions.

Accordingly Pope Paul VI has by his authority approved the **Rite of Penance** prepared by the Congregation for Divine Worship and ordered it to be published. It is to replace the pertinent sections of the **Roman Ritual** now in use. The rite in its Latin original is to come into force as soon as it is published, but vernacular versions will be effective from the day determined by the episcopal conferences, after they have approved the translation and received confirmation from the Apostolic See.

Anything to the contrary notwithstanding.

---

[2] See *AAS* 64 (1972) 510-514.

From the office of the Congregation for Divine Worship, December 2, 1973 the First Sunday of Advent.

By special mandate of the Pope

Jean Cardinal Villot
Secretary of State

✠Annibale Bugnini
Titular Archbishop of Diocletiana
Secretary of the Congregation for Divine Worship

RITE OF PENANCE

INTRODUCTION

I. THE MYSTERY OF RECONCILIATION IN THE HISTORY OF SALVATION

1.   The Father has shown forth his mercy by reconciling the world to himself in Christ and by making peace for all things on earth and in heaven by the blood of Christ on the cross.[1] The Son of God made man lived among men in order to free them from the slavery of sin[2] and to call them out of darkness into his wonderful light.[3] He therefore began his work on earth by preaching repentance and saying: "Turn away from sin and believe the good news" (Mark 1:15).

This invitation to repentance, which had often been sounded by the prophets, prepared the hearts of men for the coming of the Kingdom of God through the voice of John the Baptist who came "preaching a baptism of repentance for the forgiveness of sins" (Mark 1:4).

Jesus, however, not only exhorted men to repentance so that they should abandon their sins and turn wholeheartedly to the Lord,[4] but he also welcomed sinners and reconciled them with the Father.[5] Moreover, by healing the sick he signified his power to forgive sin.[6] Finally, he himself died for our sins and rose again for our justification.[7] Therefore, on the night he was betrayed and began his saving passion,[8] he instituted the sacrifice of the new covenant in his blood for the forgiveness of sins.[9] After his resurrection he sent the Holy Spirit upon the apostles, empowering them to forgive or retain sins[10] and sending them forth to all peoples to preach repentance and the forgiveness of sins in his name.[11]

The Lord said to Peter, "I will give you the keys of the kingdom of heaven, and whatever you bind on earth will be bound in heaven, and whatever you loose on earth will be loosed also in heaven" (Matthew 16:19). In obedience to this command, on the day of Pentecost Peter preached the forgiveness of sins by baptism: "Repent and let every one of you be baptized in the name of Jesus Christ for the forgiveness of your sins" (Acts 2:38).[12] Since then the Church has never failed to call men from sin to conversion and by the celebration of penance to show the victory of Christ over sin.

2.   This victory is first brought to light in baptism where our fallen nature is crucified with Christ so that the body of sin may be destroyed and we may no longer be slaves to sin, but rise with Christ and live for God.[13] For this reason the Church proclaims its faith in "the one baptism for the forgiveness of sins."

In the sacrifice of the Mass the passion of Christ is made present; his body given for us and his blood shed for the forgiveness of sins are offered to God again by the Church for the salvation of the world. In the eucharist Christ is present and is offered as "the sacrifice which has made our peace"[14] with God and in order that "we may be brought together in unity"[15] by his Holy Spirit.

Furthermore our Savior Jesus Christ, when he gave to his apostles and their successors power to forgive sins, instituted in his Church the sacrament of penance. Thus the faithful who fall into sin after baptism may be reconciled with God and renewed in grace.[16] The Church "possesses both water and tears: the water of baptism, the tears of penance."[17]

II. THE RECONCILIATION OF PENITENTS IN THE CHURCH'S LIFE

The Church Is Holy but Always in Need of Purification

3.   Christ "loved the Church and gave himself up for her to make her holy" (Ephesians 5:25-26), and he united the Church to himself as his bride.[18] He filled her with his divine gifts,[19] because she is his body and fullness, and through her he spreads truth and grace to all.

The members of the Church, however, are exposed to temptation and unfortunately often fall into sin. As a result, "while Christ, 'holy, innocent, and unstained' (Hebrews 7:26), did not know sin (2 Corinthians 5:21) but came only to atone for the sins of the people (see Hebrews 2:17), the Church, which includes within itself sinners and is at the same time holy and always in need of purification, constantly pursues repentance and renewal."[20]

Penance in the Church's Life and Liturgy

4.   The people of God accomplishes and perfects this continual re-pentance in many different ways. It shares in the sufferings of Christ[21] by enduring its own difficulties, carries out works of mercy and char-ity,[22] and adopts ever more fully the outlook of the Gospel message. Thus the people of God becomes in the world a sign of conversion to God. All this the Church expresses in its life and celebrates in the liturgy when the faithful confess that they are sinners and ask pardon of God and of their brothers and sisters. This happens in penitential services, in the proclamation of the word of God, in prayer, and in the penitential aspects of the eucharistic celebration.[23]

In the sacrament of penance the faithful "obtain from the mercy of God pardon for their sins against him; at the same time they are reconciled with the Church which they wounded by their sins and which works for their conversion by charity, example, and prayer."[24]

Reconciliation with God and with the Church

5.   Since every sin is an offense against God which disrupts our friendship with him, "the ultimate purpose of penance is that we should love God deeply and commit ourselves completely to him."[25] Therefore, the sinner who by the grace of a merciful God embraces the way of penance comes back to the Father who "first loved us" (1 John 4:19), to Christ who gave himself up for us,[26] and to the Holy Spirit who has been poured out on us abundantly.[27]

"By the hidden and loving mystery of God's design men are joined to-gether in the bonds of supernatural solidarity, so much so that the sin of one harms the others just as the holiness of one benefits the oth-ers."[28] Penance always entails reconciliation with our brothers and sis-ters who are always harmed by our sins.

In fact, men frequently join together to commit injustice. It is thus only fit-ting that they should help each other in doing penance so that freed from sin by the grace of Christ they may work with all men of good will for jus-tice and peace in the world.

The Sacrament of Penance and Its Parts

6.   The follower of Christ who has sinned but who has been moved by the Holy Spirit to come to the sacrament of penance should above all be

converted to God with his whole heart. This inner conversion of heart embraces sorrow for sin and the intent to lead a new life. It is expressed through confession made to the Church, due satisfaction, and amendment of life. God grants pardon for sin through the Church, which works by the ministry of priests.[29]

a)   *Contrition*

The most important act of the penitent is contrition, which is "heartfelt sorrow and aversion for the sin committed along with the intention of sinning no more."[30] "We can only approach the Kingdom of Christ by *metanoia*. This is a profound change of the whole person by which one begins to consider, judge, and arrange his life according to the holiness and love of God, made manifest in his Son in the last days and given to us in abundance" (see Hebrews 1:2; Colossians 1:19 and *passim*).[31] The genuineness of penance depends on this heartfelt contrition. For conversion should affect a person from within so that it may progressively enlighten him and render him continually more like Christ.

b)   *Confession*

The sacrament of penance includes the confession of sins, which comes from true knowledge of self before God and from contrition for those sins. However, this inner examination of heart and the exterior accusation should be made in the light of God's mercy. Confession requires in the penitent the will to open his heart to the minister of God, and in the minister a spiritual judgment by which, acting in the person of Christ, he pronounces his decision of forgiveness or retention of sins in accord with the power of the keys.[32]

c)   *Act of Penance (Satisfaction)*

True conversion is completed by acts of penance or satisfaction for the sins committed, by amendment of conduct, and also by the reparation of injury.[33] The kind and extent of the satisfaction should be suited to the personal condition of each penitent so that each one may restore the order which he disturbed and through the corresponding remedy be cured of the sickness from which he suffered. Therefore, it is necessary that the act of penance really be a remedy for sin and a help to renewal of life. Thus the penitent, "forgetting the things which are behind him"

(Philippians 3:13), again becomes part of the mystery of salvation and turns himself toward the future.

d)   Absolution

Through the sign of absolution God grants pardon to the sinner who in sacramental confession manifests his change of heart to the Church's minister, and thus the sacrament of penance is completed. In God's design the humanity and loving kindness of our Savior have visibly appeared to us,[34] and God uses visible signs to give salvation and to renew the broken covenant.

In the sacrament of penance the Father receives the repentant son who comes back to him, Christ places the lost sheep on his shoulders and brings it back to the sheepfold, and the Holy Spirit sanctifies this temple of God again or lives more fully within it. This is finally expressed in a renewed and more fervent sharing of the Lord's table, and there is great joy at the banquet of God's Church over the son who has returned from afar.[35]

The Necessity and Benefit of the Sacrament

7.   Just as the wound of sin is varied and multiple in the life of individuals and of the community, so too the healing which penance provides is varied. Those who by grave sin have withdrawn from the communion of love with God are called back in the sacrament of penance to the life they have lost. And those who through daily weakness fall into venial sins draw strength from a repeated celebration of penance to gain the full freedom of the children of God.

a)   To obtain the saving remedy of the sacrament of penance, according to the plan of our merciful God, the faithful must confess to a priest each and every grave sin which they remember upon examination of their conscience.[36]

b)   Moreover, frequent and careful celebration of this sacrament is also very useful as a remedy for venial sins. This is not a mere ritual repetition or psychological exercise, but a serious striving to perfect the grace of baptism so that, as we bear in our body the death of Jesus Christ, his life may be seen in us ever more clearly.[37] In confession of this kind, penitents who accuse themselves of venial faults should try to conform more closely to Christ and to follow the voice of the Spirit more attentively.

In order that this sacrament of healing may truly achieve its purpose among Christ's faithful, it must take root in their whole lives and move them to more fervent service of God and neighbor.

The celebration of this sacrament is thus always an act in which the Church proclaims its faith, gives thanks to God for the freedom with which Christ has made us free,[38] and offers its life as a spiritual sacrifice in praise of God's glory, as it hastens to meet the Lord Jesus.

III. OFFICES AND MINISTRIES IN THE RECONCILIATION OF PENITENTS

The Community in the Celebration of Penance

8.   The whole Church, as a priestly people, acts in different ways in the work of reconciliation which has been entrusted to it by the Lord. Not only does the Church call sinners to repentance by preaching the word of God, but it also intercedes for them and helps penitents with maternal care and solicitude to acknowledge and admit their sins and so obtain the mercy of God who alone can forgive sins. Furthermore, the Church becomes the instrument of the conversion and absolution of the penitent through the ministry entrusted by Christ to the apostles and their successors.[39]

9.   *The Minister of the Sacrament of Penance*

a)   The Church exercises the ministry of the sacrament of penance through bishops and priests. By preaching God's word they call the faithful to conversion; in the name of Christ and by the power of the Holy Spirit they declare and grant the forgiveness of sins.

In the exercise of this ministry priests act in communion with the bishop and share in his power and office of regulating the penitential discipline.[40]

b)   The competent minister of the sacrament of penance is a priest who has the faculty to absolve in accordance with the provisions of the Code of Canon Law, canons 967-975. All priests, however, even though not approved to hear confessions, absolve validly and lawfully any penitents without exception who are in danger of death.

10. *The Pastoral Exercise of This Ministry*

a)   In order to fulfill his ministry properly and faithfully the confessor should understand the disorders of souls and apply the appropriate remedies to them. He should fulfill his office of judge wisely and should acquire the knowledge and prudence necessary for this task by serious study, guided by the teaching authority of the Church and especially by fervent prayer to God. Discernment of spirits is a deep knowledge of God's action in the hearts of men; it is a gift of the Spirit as well as the fruit of charity.[41]

b)   The confessor should always be ready and willing to hear the confessions of the faithful when they make a reasonable request of him.[42]

c)   By receiving the repentant sinner and leading him to the light of the truth the confessor fulfills a paternal function: he reveals the heart of the Father and shows the image of Christ the Good Shepherd. He should keep in mind that he has been entrusted with the ministry of Christ, who mercifully accomplished the saving work of man's redemption and who is present by his power in the sacraments.[43]

d)   As the minister of God the confessor comes to know the secrets of another's conscience, and he is bound to keep the sacramental seal of confession absolutely inviolate.

The Penitent

11.   The acts of the penitent in the celebration of the sacrament are of the greatest importance.

When with proper dispositions he approaches this saving remedy instituted by Christ and confesses his sins, he shares by his actions in the sacrament itself; the sacrament is completed when the words of absolution are spoken by the minister in the name of Christ.

Thus the faithful Christian, as he experiences and proclaims the mercy of God in his life, celebrates with the priest the liturgy by which the Church continually renews itself.

IV. THE CELEBRATION OF THE SACRAMENT OF PENANCE

The Place of Celebration

12.   The sacrament of penance is ordinarily celebrated in a church or oratory, unless a legitimate reason stands in the way.

The episcopal conferences are to establish the norms pertaining to the confessional, which will include provision for clearly visible confessionals that the faithful who wish may readily use and that are equipped with a fixed screen between the penitent and the confessor.

Except for a legitimate reason, confessions are not to be heard outside a confessional.[44]

The Time of Celebration

13.   The reconciliation of penitents may be celebrated at any time on any day, but it is desirable that the faithful know the day and time at which the priest is available for this ministry. They should be encouraged to approach the sacrament of penance at times when Mass is not being celebrated and especially during the scheduled periods.[45]

The season of Lent is most appropriate for celebrating the sacrament of penance. Already on Ash Wednesday the people of God has heard the solemn invitation "Turn away from sin and believe the good news." It is therefore fitting to have several penitential celebrations during Lent, so that all the faithful may have an opportunity to be reconciled with God and their neighbor and so be able to celebrate the paschal mystery in the Easter triduum with renewed hearts.

Liturgical Vestments

14. The regulations laid down by the local Ordinaries for the use of liturgical vestments in the celebration of penance are to be observed.

A. Rite for the Reconciliation of Individual Penitents

Preparation of Priest and Penitent

15.   Priest and penitent should first prepare themselves by prayer to celebrate the sacrament. The priest should call upon the Holy Spirit so that he

may receive enlightenment and charity. The penitent should compare his life with the example and commandments of Christ and then pray to God for the forgiveness of his sins.

Welcoming the Penitent

16.   The priest should welcome the penitent with fraternal charity and, if the occasion permits, address him with friendly words. The penitent then makes the sign of the cross, saying: "In the name of the Father, and of the Son, and of the Holy Spirit. Amen." The priest may also make the sign of the cross with the penitent. Next the priest briefly urges the penitent to have confidence in God. If the penitent is unknown to the priest, it is proper for him to indicate his state in life, the time of his last confession, his difficulties in leading the Christian life, and anything else which may help the confessor in exercising his ministry.

Reading the Word of God

17.   Then the priest, or the penitent himself, may read a text of holy Scripture, or this may be done as part of the preparation for the sacrament. Through the word of God the Christian receives light to recognize his sins and is called to conversion and to confidence in God's mercy.

Confession of Sins and the Act of Penance

18. The penitent then confesses his sins, beginning, where customary, with a form of general confession: *I confess to almighty God.* If necessary, the priest should help the penitent to make a complete confession; he should also encourage him to have sincere sorrow for his sins against God. Finally, the priest should offer suitable counsel to help the penitent begin a new life and, where necessary, instruct him in the duties of the Christian way of life.

If the penitent has been the cause of harm or scandal to others, the priest should lead him to resolve that he will make appropriate restitution.

Then the priest imposes an act of penance or satisfaction on the penitent; this should serve not only to make up for the past but also to help him to begin a new life and provide him with an antidote to weakness. As far as possible, the penance should correspond to the seriousness and nature of the sins. This act of penance may suitably take the form of prayer, self-denial, and especially service of one's neighbor and works of mercy. These will underline the fact that sin and its forgiveness have a social aspect.

The Prayer of the Penitent and the Absolution by the Priest

19. After this the penitent manifests his contrition and resolution to begin a new life by means of a prayer for God's pardon. It is desirable that this prayer should be based on the words of Scripture.

Following this prayer, the priest extends his hands, or at least his right hand, over the head of the penitent and pronounces the formula of absolution, in which the essential words are: "I absolve you from your sins in the name of the Father and of the Son and of the Holy Spirit." As he says the final words the priest makes the sign of the cross over the penitent. The form of absolution (see no. 46) indicates that the reconciliation of the penitent comes from the mercy of the Father; it shows the connection between the reconciliation of the sinner and the paschal mystery of Christ; it stresses the role of the Holy Spirit in the forgiveness of sins; finally, it underlines the ecclesial aspect of the sacrament because reconciliation with God is asked for and given through the ministry of the Church.

Proclamation of Praise and Dismissal of the Penitent

20. After receiving pardon for his sins the penitent praises the mercy of God and gives him thanks in a short invocation taken from scripture. Then the priest tells him to go in peace.

The penitent continues his conversion and expresses it by a life renewed according to the Gospel and more and more steeped in the love of God, for "love covers over a multitude of sins" (1 Peter 4:8).

Short Rite

21. When pastoral need dictates it, the priest may omit or shorten some parts of the rite but must always retain in their entirety the confession of sins and the acceptance of the act of penance, the invitation to contrition (no. 44), and the form of absolution and the dismissal. In imminent danger of death, it is sufficient for the priest to say the essential words of the form of absolution, namely, "I absolve you from your sins in the name of the Father, and of the Son, and of the Holy Spirit."

B. Rite for Reconciliation of Several Penitents with Individual Confession and Absolution

22. When a number of penitents assemble at the same time to receive sacramental reconciliation, it is fitting that they be prepared for the sacrament by a celebration of the word of God.

Those who will receive the sacrament at another time may also take part in the service.

Communal celebration shows more clearly the ecclesial nature of penance. The faithful listen together to the word of God, which proclaims his mercy and invites them to conversion; at the same time they examine the conformity of their lives with that word of God and help each other through common prayer. After each person has confessed his sins and received absolution, all praise God together for his wonderful deeds on behalf of the people he has gained for himself through the blood of his Son.

If necessary, several priests should be available in suitable places to hear individual confessions and to reconcile the penitents.

Introductory Rites

23. When the faithful are assembled, a suitable hymn may be sung. Then the priest greets them, and, if necessary, he or another minister gives a brief introduction to the celebration and explains the order of service. Next he invites all to pray and after a period of silence completes the (opening) prayer.

The Celebration of the Word of God

24. The sacrament of penance should begin with a hearing of God's word, because through his word God calls men to repentance and leads them to a true conversion of heart.

One or more readings may be chosen. If more than one are read, a psalm, another suitable song, or a period of silence should be inserted between them, so that the word of God may be more deeply understood and heartfelt assent may be given to it. If there is only one reading, it is preferable that it be from the gospel.

Readings should be chosen which illustrate the following:

a)   the voice of God calling men back to conversion and ever closer conformity with Christ;

b)   the mystery of our reconciliation through the death and resurrection of Christ and through the gift of the Holy Spirit;

c)   the judgment of God about good and evil in men's lives as a help in the examination of conscience.

25.   The homily, taking its theme from the scriptural text, should lead the penitents to examine their consciences and to turn away from sin and toward God. It should remind the faithful that sin works against God, against the community and one's neighbors, and against the sinner himself. Therefore, it would be good to recall:

a)   the infinite mercy of God, greater than all our sins, by which again and again he calls us back to himself;

b)   the need for interior repentance, by which we are genuinely prepared to make reparation for sin;

c)   the social aspect of grace and sin, by which the actions of individuals in some degree affect the whole body of the Church;

d)   the duty to make satisfaction for sin, which is effective because of Christ's work of reparation and requires especially, in addition to works of penance, the exercise of true charity toward God and neighbor.

26.   After the homily a suitable period of silence should be allowed for examining one's conscience and awakening true contrition for sin. The priest or a deacon or other minister may help the faithful with brief considerations or a litany, adapted to their background, age, etc.

If it is judged suitable, this communal examination of conscience and awakening of contrition may take the place of the homily. But in this case it should be clearly based on the text of scripture that has just been read.

The Rite of Reconciliation

27.   At the invitation of the deacon or other minister, all kneel or bow their heads and say a form of general confession (for example, *I confess to almighty God*). Then they stand and join in a litany or suitable song to ex-

press confession of sins, heartfelt contrition, prayer for forgiveness, and trust in God's mercy. Finally, they say the Lord's Prayer, which is never omitted.

28.   After the Lord's Prayer the priests go to the places assigned for confession. The penitents who desire to confess their sins go to the priest of their choice. After receiving a suitable act of penance, they are absolved by him with the form for the reconciliation of an individual penitent.

29.   When the confessions are over, the priests return to the sanctuary. The priest who presides invites all to make an act of thanksgiving and to praise God for his mercy. This may be done in a psalm or hymn or litany. Finally, the priest concludes the celebration with prayer, praising God for the great love he has shown us.

Dismissal of the People

30.   After the prayer of thanksgiving the priest blesses the faithful. Then the deacon or the priest himself dismisses the congregation.

C. Rite for Reconciliation of Penitents with General Confession and Absolution

The Discipline of General Absolution

31.   An individual, complete confession and the receiving of absolution constitute the sole, ordinary means for a member of the faithful who is conscious of serious sin to be reconciled with God and the Church. Physical or moral impossibility alone excuses from this kind of confession; in the case of such impossibility, reconciliation is possible in other ways.

Absolution without prior, individual confession cannot be given collectively to a number of penitents unless:

a)   the danger of death is imminent and there is no time for a priest or priests to hear the confessions of the individual penitents;

b)   a serious need is present, namely, given the number of penitents, not enough confessors are available to hear the individual confessions properly within a reasonable time, with the result that through no fault of their own, the faithful would be forced to be for a long time without the grace of the sacrament or without communion. The need in question is not regarded as sufficient when the nonavailability of confessors is based solely on there being a large number of penitents, such as may be the case at some great festival or pilgrimage.[46]

32.   To make the judgment on whether the requisite conditions already stated in no. 31[b] are verified belongs to the diocesan bishop. After considering the criteria agreed on with the other members of the episcopal conference, he can decide which cases involve the need in question.[47]

33.   For the valid reception of general sacramental absolution it is required that the faithful not only be properly disposed but at the same time have the resolution to confess in due time each of those serious sins that they cannot at the present time confess in this way.

On the occasion of the reception of general absolution, the faithful, to the extent possible, are to be instructed on the requirements just mentioned; even in the case of danger of death when time allows, the imparting of general absolution is to be preceded by an exhortation that each recipient strive to make an act of contrition.[48]

34.   Unless there is a good reason preventing it, those who receive pardon for serious sins through general absolution are to go to individual confession as soon as they have the opportunity before any further reception of general absolution. And unless a moral impossibility stands in the way, they are absolutely bound to go to a confessor within one year. For the precept binding every one of the faithful binds them as well, namely, to confess individually to a priest at least once a year all those grave sins not hitherto confessed one by one.[49]

The Rite of General Absolution

35.   For the reconciliation of penitents by general confession and absolution in the cases provided by law, everything takes place as described above for the reconciliation of several penitents with individual confession and absolution, with the following exceptions:

a)   After the homily or during it, the faithful who seek general absolution should be instructed to dispose themselves properly, that is, each one should be sorry for his sins and resolve to avoid committing them again. He should intend to repair any scandal and harm he may have caused and likewise resolve to confess in due time each one of the grave sins which cannot be confessed at present.[50] Some act of penance should be proposed for all; individuals may add to this penance if they wish.

b)   The deacon, another minister, or the priest then calls upon the penitents who wish to receive absolution to show their intention by some sign (for example, by bowing their heads, kneeling, or giving some other sign determined by the episcopal conferences). They should also say together a form of general confession (for example, I confess to almighty God), which may be followed by a litany or a penitential song. Then the Lord's Prayer is sung or said by all, as indicated in no. 27, above.

c)   Then the priest calls upon the grace of the Holy Spirit for the forgiveness of sins, proclaims the victory over sin of Christ's death and resurrection, and gives sacramental absolution to the penitents.

d)   Finally, the priest invites the people to give thanks, as described in no. 29, above, and, omitting the concluding prayer, he immediately blesses and dismisses them.

V. PENITENTIAL CELEBRATIONS

Nature and Structure

36.   Penitential celebrations are gatherings of the people of God to hear the proclamation of God's word. This invites them to conversion and renewal of life and announces our freedom from sin through the death and resurrection of Christ. The structure of these services is the same as that usually followed in celebrations of the word of God[51] and given in the *Rite of Reconciliation of Several Penitents.*

It is appropriate, therefore, that after the introductory rites (song, greeting, and prayer) one or more biblical readings be chosen with songs, psalms, or periods of silence inserted between them. In the homily these readings should be explained and applied to the congregation. Before or after the readings from scripture, readings from the Fathers or other writers may be selected which will help the community and each person to a true awareness of sin and heartfelt sorrow, in other words, to bring about conversion of life.

After the homily and reflection on God's word, it is desirable that the congregation, united in voice and spirit, pray together in a litany or in some other way suited to general participation. At the end the Lord's Prayer is said, asking God our Father "to forgive us our sins as we forgive those who sin against us . . . and deliver us from evil." The priest or the minister who presides concludes with a prayer and the dismissal of the people.

Benefit and Importance

37.   Care should be taken that the faithful do not confuse these celebrations with the celebration of the sacrament of penance.[52] Penitential celebrations are very helpful in promoting conversion of life and purification of heart.[53]

It is desirable to arrange such services especially for these purposes:

—to foster the spirit of penance within the Christian community;

—to help the faithful to prepare for confession which can be made individually later at a convenient time;

—to help children gradually to form their conscience about sin in human life and about freedom from sin through Christ;

—to help catechumens during their conversion.

Penitential celebrations, moreover, are very useful in places where no priest is available to give sacramental absolution. They offer help in reaching that perfect contrition which comes from charity and enables the faithful to attain to God's grace through a desire for the sacrament of penance.[54]

VI. ADAPTATIONS OF THE RITE TO VARIOUS REGIONS AND CIRCUMSTANCES

Adaptations by the Episcopal Conferences

38.   In preparing particular rituals the episcopal conferences may adapt the rite of penance to the needs of individual regions so that after confirmation by the Apostolic See the rituals may be used in the respective regions. It is the responsibility of the episcopal conferences in this matter:

a)   to establish regulations for the discipline of the sacrament of penance, particularly those affecting the ministry of priests;

b)   to determine more precisely regulations about the confessional for the ordinary celebration of the sacrament of penance (see no. 12) and about the signs of repentance to be shown by the faithful before general absolution (see no. 35);

c)   to prepare translations of texts adapted to the character and language of each people and also to compose new texts for the prayers of the faithful and the minister, keeping sacramental formulary intact.

The Competence of the Bishop

39.   It is for the diocesan bishop:

a)   to regulate the discipline of penance in his diocese,[55] including adaptations of the rite according to the rules proposed by the episcopal conferences;

b)   to make the decision, after considering the conditions required by the law (see no. 31[b]) and the criteria agreed on with the other members of the episcopal conference, regarding the cases of need in which general absolution may be permitted.[56]

Adaptations by the Minister

40.   It is for priests, and especially parish priests (pastors):

a)   in celebrating, to adapt the rite to the concrete circumstances of the penitents. The essential structure and the entire form of absolution must be kept, but if necessary they may omit some parts for pastoral reasons or enlarge upon them, may select the texts of readings or prayers, and may choose a place more suitable for the celebration according to the regulations of the episcopal conference, so that the entire celebration may be enriching and effective;

b)   to schedule and prepare occasional penitential celebrations during the year, especially in Lent. In order that the texts chosen and the order of the celebration may be adapted to the conditions and circumstances of the community or group (for example, children, sick persons, etc.), they may be assisted by others, including the laity.

NOTES

1. See 2 Corinthians 5:18ff; Colossians 1:20.
2. See John 8:34-36.
3. See 1 Peter 2:9.
4. See Luke 15.
5. Luke 5:20, 27-32; 7:48.
6. See Matthew 9:2-8.
7. See Romans 4:25.
8. See Roman Missal, Eucharistic Prayer III.
9. See Matthew 26:28.
10. See John 20:19-23.
11. See Luke 24:47.
12. See Acts 3:19, 26; 17:30.
13. See Romans 6:4-10.
14. Roman Missal, Eucharistic Prayer III.
15. Roman Missal, Eucharistic Prayer II.
16. See Council of Trent, Session XIV, De sacramento Paenitentiae, Chapter 1: Denz.-Schön. 1668 and 1670; can. 1: Denz.-Schön. 1701.
17. St. Ambrose, Letter 41:12: *PL* 16, 1116.
18. See Revelation 19:7.
19. See Ephesians 1:22-23; Second Vatican Council, constitution *Lumen gentium*, no. 7: *AAS* 57 (1965) 9-11.
20. Second Vatican Council, constitution *Lumen gentium*, no. 8: *ibid.*, 12.
21. See 1 Peter 4:13.
22. See 1 Peter 4:8.
23. See Council of Trent, Session XIV, De sacramento Paenitentiae: Denz.-Schön. 1638, 1740, 1743; Congregation of Rites, instruction *Eucharisticum mysterium*, May 25, 1967, no. 35: *AAS* 59 (1967) 560-561; Roman Missal, *General Instruction*, nos. 29, 30, 56 a. b. g.
24. Second Vatican Council, constitution *Lumen gentium*, no. 11: *AAS* 57 (1965) 15-16.
25. Paul VI, Apostolic Constitution *Paenitemini*, February 17, 1966: *AAS* 58 (1966) 179; see Second Vatican Council, constitution *Lumen gentium*, no. 11: *AAS* 57 (1965) 15-16.
26. See Galatians 2:20; Ephesians 5:25.
27. See Titus 3:6.
28. Paul VI, Apostolic Constitution *Indulgentiarum doctrina*, January 1, 1967, no. 4: *AAS* 59 (1967) 9; see Pius XII, encyclical *Mystici Corporis*, June 29, 1943: *AAS* 35 (1943) 213.
29. See Council of Trent, Session XIV, De sacramento Paenitentiae, Chapter 1: Denz.-Schön. 1673-1675.
30. *Ibid.*, Chapter 4: Denz.-Schön. 1676.

31. Paul VI, Apostolic Constitution *Paenitemini*, February 17, 1966: *AAS* 58 (1966) 179.

32. See Council of Trent, Session XIV, De sacramento Paenitentiae, Chapter 5: Denz.-Schön. 1679.

33. See Council of Trent, Session XIV, De sacramento Paenitentiae, Chapter 8: Denz.-Schön. 1690-1692, Paul VI, Apostolic Constitution *Indulgentiarum doctrina*, January 1, 1967, nos. 2-3: *AAS* 59 (1967) 6-8.

34. See Titus 3:4-5.

35. See Luke 15:7, 10, 32.

36. See Council of Trent, Session XIV, De sacramento Paenitentiae, can. 7-8: Denz.-Schön. 1707-1708.

37. See 2 Corinthians 4:10.

38. See Galatians 4:31.

39. See Matthew 18:18; John 20:23.

40. See Second Vatican Council, constitution *Lumen gentium*, no. 26: *AAS* 57 (1965) 31-32.

41. See Philippians 1:9-10.

42. See Congregation for the Doctrine of the Faith, *Normae pastorales circa absolutionem sacramentalem generali modo impertiendam*, June 16, 1972, no. XII: *AAS* 64 (1972) 514.

43. See Second Vatican Council, constitution *Sacrosanctum Concilium*, no. 7: *AAS* 56 (1964) 100-101.

44. See CIC, can. 964.

45. See Congregation of Rites, instruction *Eucharisticum mysterium*, May 25, 1967, no. 35: *AAS* 59 (1967) 560-561.

46. See CIC, can. 960 and 961, §1.

47. See CIC, can. 961, §2.

48. See CIC, can. 962, §§1 and 2.

49. See Congregation for the Doctrine of Faith, *Normae pastorales circa absolutionem sacramentalem generali modo impertiendam*, June 16, 1972, nos. VII and VIII: *AAS* 64 (1972) 512-513. CIC, can. 963, 989.

50. See *ibid.*, no. VI *loc. cit.*, 512.

51. See Congregation of Rites, instruction *Inter Oecumenici*, September 26, 1964, nos. 37-39: *AAS* 56 (1964) 110-111.

52. See Congregation for the Doctrine of the Faith, *Normae pastorales circa absolutionem sacramentalem generali modo impertiendam*, June 16, 1972, no. X: *AAS* 64 (1972) 513-514.

53. *Ibid.*

54. See Council of Trent, Session XIV. *De sacramento Paenitentiae*, chapter 5: Denz.-Schön. 1677.

55. See Second Vatican Council, constitution *Lumen gentium*, no. 26: *AAS* 57 (1965) 31-32.

56. See Congregation for the Doctrine of the Faith, *Normae pastorales circa absolutionem sacramentalem generali modo impertiendam*, June 16, 1972, no. V: *AAS* 64 (1972) 512. CIC, can. 961, §§1 and 2.

CHAPTER I

RITE FOR RECONCILIATION
OF
INDIVIDUAL PENITENTS

OUTLINE

Reception of the Penitent
  Greeting
  Sign of the Cross
  Invitation to Trust in God

Reading of the Word of God

Confession of Sins and Acceptance of Satisfaction

Prayer of the Penitent and Absolution

Proclamation of Praise of God and Dismissal

RITE FOR RECONCILIATION OF INDIVIDUAL PENITENTS

RECEPTION OF THE PENITENT

41. When the penitent comes to confess his sins, the priest welcomes him warmly and greets him with kindness.

42. Then the penitent makes the sign of the cross which the priest may make also.

In the name of the Father, and of the Son, and of the Holy Spirit. Amen.

The priest invites the penitent to have trust in God, in these or similar words:

1

May God, who has enlightened every heart,
help you to know your sins
and trust in his mercy.

The penitent answers:

Amen.

2
[67]

The Lord does not wish the sinner to die   (Ezekiel 33:11)
but to turn back to him and live.
Come before him with trust in his mercy.

3
[68]

May the Lord Jesus welcome you.   (Luke 5:32)
He came to call sinners, not the just.
Have confidence in him.

4
[69]

May the grace of the Holy Spirit
fill your heart with light,
that you may confess your sins with loving trust
and come to know that God is merciful.

5   [70]

May the Lord be in your heart
and help you to confess your sins with true sorrow.

6   [71]

If you have sinned do not lose heart.   (1 John 2:1-2)
We have Jesus Christ to plead for us with the Father:
he is the holy One,
the atonement for our sins
and for the sins of the whole world.

READING OF THE WORD OF GOD (Optional)

> 43. Then the priest may read or say from memory a text of Scripture which proclaims God's mercy and calls man to conversion.

1   [73]

Listen to what the Lord says to us: Ezekiel 11:19-20
I will give them a new heart
    and put a new spirit within them;
    I will remove the stony heart from their bodies,
    and replace it with a natural heart,
    so that they will live according to my statutes,
    and observe and carry out my ordinances;
    thus they shall be my people and I will be their God.

2   [74]

Listen to what the Lord says to us: Matthew 6:14-15
"If you forgive men their transgressions,
    your heavenly Father will forgive you.
But if you do not forgive men,
    neither will your Father forgive your transgressions."

3   [75]

After John had been arrested,   Mark 1:14-15
    Jesus came to Galilee proclaiming the Gospel of God:
    "This is the time of fulfillment.

The Kingdom of God is at hand.
Repent, and believe in the Gospel."

4   [79]

God proves his love for us   Romans 5:8-9
    in that while we were still sinners Christ died for us.
How much more then, since we are now justified by his
    blood,
    will we be saved through him from the wrath.

5   [80]

Ephesians 5:1-2

So be imitators of God, as beloved children, and live in
    love,
    as Christ loved us and handed himself over for us
    as a sacrificial offering to God for a fragrant aroma.

6   [83]

If we say, "We have fellowship with him,"   1 John 1:6-7, 9
    while we continue to walk in darkness,
    we lie and do not act in truth.
But if we walk in the light as he is in the light,
    then we have fellowship with one another,
    and the Blood of his Son Jesus cleanses us from all
    sin.
If we acknowledge our sins, he is faithful and just
    and will forgive our sins and cleanse us from every
    wrongdoing.

> A reading may also be chosen from those given in nos. 101-201
> (page **89**), and nos. 72-82 (page **78**) for the reconciliation of several
> penitents. The priest and penitent may choose other readings from
> scripture.

CONFESSION OF SINS AND ACCEPTANCE OF SATISFACTION

44. Where it is the custom, the penitent says a general formula for confession (for example, **I confess to almighty God**) before he confesses his sins.

If necessary, the priest helps the penitent to make an integral confession and gives him suitable counsel. He urges him to be sorry for his faults, reminding him that through the sacrament of penance the Christian dies and rises with Christ and is thus renewed in the paschal mystery. The priest proposes an act of penance which the penitent accepts to make satisfaction for sin and to amend his life.

The priest should make sure that he adapts his counsel to the penitent's circumstances.

PRAYER OF THE PENITENT AND ABSOLUTION

45. The priest then asks the penitent to express his sorrow, which the penitent may do in these or similar words:

1

My God,
I am sorry for my sins with all my heart.
In choosing to do wrong
and failing to do good,
I have sinned against you
whom I should love above all things.
I firmly intend, with your help,
to do penance,
to sin no more,
and to avoid whatever leads me to sin.
Our Savior Jesus Christ
suffered and died for us.
In his name, my God, have mercy.

2 [85]

Remember that your compassion, O L<small>ORD</small>, Psalm 25:6-7
    and your love are from of old.
In your kindness remember me,
    because of your goodness, O L<small>ORD</small>.

3 [86]

Thoroughly wash me from my guilt Psalm 51:4-5
    and of my sin cleanse me.
For I acknowledge my offense,
    and my sin is before me always.

4 [87]

Father, I have sinned [. . .] against you. Luke 15:18; 18:13
I no longer deserve to be called your son.
Be merciful to me a sinner.

5 [88]

Father of mercy,
like the prodigal son
I return to you and say:
"I have sinned against you
and am no longer worthy to be called your son."
Christ Jesus, Savior of the world,
I pray with the repentant thief
to whom you promised Paradise:
"Lord, remember me in your kingdom."
Holy Spirit, fountain of love,
I call on you with trust:
"Purify my heart,
and help me to walk as a child of light."

6   [89]

Lord Jesus,
you opened the eyes of the blind,
healed the sick,
forgave the sinful woman,
and after Peter's denial confirmed him in your love.
Listen to my prayer:
forgive all my sins,
renew your love in my heart,
help me to live in perfect unity with my fellow Christians
that I may proclaim your saving power to all the world.

7   [90]

Lord Jesus,
you chose to be called the friend of sinners.
By your saving death and resurrection
free me from my sins.
May your peace take root in my heart
and bring forth a harvest
of love, holiness, and truth.

8   [91]

Lord Jesus Christ,
you are the Lamb of God;
you take away the sins of the world.
Through the grace of the Holy Spirit
restore me to friendship with your Father,
cleanse me from every stain of sin
in the blood you shed for me,
and raise me to new life
for the glory of your name.

9

Lord God,   [92]
in your goodness have mercy on me:

do not look on my sins,
but take away all my guilt.
Create in me a clean heart
and renew within me an upright spirit.

1

10

Lord Jesus, Son of God,
have mercy on me, a sinner.

> 46. Then the priest extends his hands over the penitent's head (or at least extends his right hand) and says:

God, the Father of mercies,
through the death and resurrection of his Son
has reconciled the world to himself
and sent the Holy Spirit among us
for the forgiveness of sins;
through the ministry of the Church
may God give you pardon and peace,
and I absolve you from your sins
in the name of the Father, and of the Son, ✠
and of the Holy Spirit.

> The penitent answers:

Amen.

PROCLAMATION OF PRAISE OF GOD AND DISMISSAL

> 47. After the absolution, the priest continues:

1

Give thanks to the Lord, for he is good.

> The penitent concludes:

His mercy endures for ever.

> Then the priest dismisses the penitent who has been reconciled, saying:

The Lord has freed you from your sins. Go in peace.

2

[93]

May the Passion of our Lord Jesus Christ,
the intercession of the Blessed Virgin and of all the
  saints,
whatever good you do and suffering you endure,
heal your sins,
help you to grow in holiness,
and reward you with eternal life.
Go in peace.

3

The Lord has freed you from sin.
May he bring you safely to his kingdom in heaven.
Glory to him for ever.
  ℟. Amen.

4

Blessed are those
whose sins have been forgiven,
whose evil deeds have been forgotten.
Rejoice in the Lord,
and go in peace.

5

Go in peace,
and proclaim to the world
the wonderful works of God,
who has brought you salvation.

CHAPTER II

RITE FOR RECONCILIATION OF SEVERAL PENITENTS WITH INDIVIDUAL CONFESSION AND ABSOLUTION

2

OUTLINE

INTRODUCTORY RITES

Song
Greeting
Introduction
Opening Prayer

CELEBRATION OF THE WORD OF GOD

First Reading
Responsorial Psalm
Second Reading
Gospel Acclamation
Gospel
Homily
Examination of Conscience

RITE OF RECONCILIATION

General Confession of Sins
Litany or Song
Lord's Prayer
Individual Confession and Absolution
Proclamation of Praise for God's Mercy
Concluding Prayer of Thanksgiving

CONCLUDING RITE

Blessing
Dismissal

RITE FOR RECONCILIATION OF SEVERAL PENITENTS WITH INDIVIDUAL CONFESSION AND ABSOLUTION

INTRODUCTORY RITES

SONG

48. When the faithful have assembled, they may sing a psalm, antiphon, or other appropriate song while the priest is entering the church, for example:

1

Hear us, Lord,
for you are merciful and kind.
In your great compassion,
look on us with love.

2

Let us come with confidence before the throne of grace
to receive God's mercy,
and we shall find pardon and strength
in our time of need.

GREETING

49. After the song the priest greets the congregation:

1

Grace, mercy, and peace be with you
from God the Father
and Christ Jesus our Savior.
   R̷. And also with you.

2

Grace and peace be with you
from God the Father
and from Jesus Christ
who loved us
and washed away our sins in his blood.

℟. Glory to him for ever. Amen.

3   [94]

Grace, mercy, and peace
from God the Father and Jesus Christ his Son
be with you in truth and love.

℟. Amen.

4   [95]

May God open your hearts to his law
and give you peace;
may he answer your prayers
and restore you to friendship.

℟. Amen.

5   [96]

Grace and peace with you
from God our Father
and from the Lord Jesus Christ
who laid down his life for our sins.

℟. Glory to him for ever. Amen.

Then the priest or another minister speaks briefly about the importance and purpose of the celebration and the order of the service.

OPENING PRAYER

50. The priest invites all to pray, using these or similar words:

Brothers and sisters, God calls us to conversion; let us therefore ask him for the grace of sincere repentance.

All pray in silence for a brief period. Then the priest sings or says the prayer:

1

Lord,
hear the prayers of those who call on you,
forgive the sins of those who confess to you,
and in your merciful love
give us your pardon and your peace.
We ask this through Christ our Lord.

℟. Amen.

2

Lord,
send your Spirit among us
to cleanse us in the waters of repentance.
May he make of us a living sacrifice
so that in every place,
by his life-giving power,
we may praise your glory
and proclaim your loving compassion.
We ask this through Christ our Lord.

℟. Amen.

3

Lord   [97]
turn to us in mercy
and forgive us all our sins
that we may serve you in true freedom.
We ask this through Christ our Lord.

℟. Amen.

4   [98]

Lord our God
you are patient with sinners
and accept our desire to make amends.
We acknowledge our sins
and are resolved to change our lives.
Help us to celebrate this sacrament of your mercy
so that we may reform our lives
and receive from you the gift of everlasting joy.
We ask this through Christ our Lord.

℞. Amen.

5   [99]

Almighty and merciful God,
you have brought us together in the name of your Son
to receive your mercy and grace in our time of need.
Open our eyes to see the evil we have done.
Touch our hearts and convert us to yourself.
Where sin has divided and scattered,
may your love make one again;
where sin has brought weakness,
may your power heal and strengthen;
where sin has brought death,
may your Spirit raise to new life.

Give us a new heart to love you,
so that our lives may reflect the image of your Son.
May the world see the glory of Christ
revealed in your Church,
and come to know
that he is the one whom you have sent,
Jesus Christ, your Son, our Lord.

℞. Amen.

6   [100]

Father of mercies
and God of all consolation,
you do not wish the sinner to die
but to be converted and live.
Come to the aid of your people,
that they may turn from their sins
and live for you alone.
May we be attentive to your word,
confess our sins, receive your forgiveness,
and be always grateful for your loving kindness.
Help us to live the truth in love
and grow into the fullness of Christ, your Son,
who lives and reigns for ever and ever.

> R⁊. Amen.

CELEBRATION OF THE WORD OF GOD

51. The celebration of the word follows. If there are several readings a psalm or other appropriate song or even a period of silence should intervene between them, so that everyone may understand the word of God more deeply and give it his heartfelt assent. If there is only one reading, it is preferable that it be from the gospel.

FIRST EXAMPLE

Love is the fullness of the law

FIRST READING   Deuteronomy 5:1-3, 6-7, 11-12, 16-21a; 6:4-6

A reading from the Book of Deuteronomy

Love the Lord your God with all your heart.

Moses summoned all Israel and said to them, "Hear, O Israel, the statutes and decrees which I proclaim in your hearing this day, that you may learn them and take care to observe them. The LORD, our God, made a covenant with us at

Horeb; not with our fathers did he make this covenant, but with us, all of us who are alive here this day. He said:

"'I, the LORD, am your God, who brought you out of the land of Egypt, that place of slavery. You shall not have other gods besides me.

"'You shall not take the name of the LORD, your God, in vain. For the LORD will not leave unpunished him who takes his name in vain.

"'Take care to keep holy the sabbath day as the LORD, your God, commanded you.

"'Honor your father and your mother, as the LORD, your God, has commanded you, that you may have a long life and prosperity in the land which the LORD, your God, is giving you.

"'You shall not kill.

"'You shall not commit adultery.

"'You shall not steal.

"'You shall not bear dishonest witness against your neighbor.

"'You shall not covet your neighbor's wife.'

"Hear, O Israel! The LORD is our God, the LORD alone! Therefore, you shall love the LORD, your God, with all your heart, and with all your soul, and with all your strength. Take to heart these words which I enjoin on you today."

The word of the Lord.

RESPONSORIAL PSALM   Baruch 1:15-22

℞. (3, 2) Listen and have pity, Lord, because you are merciful.

Justice is with the LORD, our God;
    and we today are flushed with shame,

That we have sinned in the Lord's sight
  and disobeyed him.

  ℟. Listen and have pity, Lord, because you are merciful.

We have neither heeded the voice of the Lord, our God,
  nor followed the precepts which the Lord set before us.
We have been disobedient to the Lord, our God,
  and only too ready to disregard his voice.

  ℟. Listen and have pity, Lord, because you are merciful.

We did not heed
  the voice of the Lord, our God,
But each one of us went off after the devices of our own
    wicked hearts,
  and did evil in the sight of the Lord, our God.

  ℟. Listen and have pity, Lord, because you are merciful.

2

SECOND READING   Ephesians 5:1-14

A reading from the Letter of Saint Paul to the Ephesians

You were once darkness, but now you are light in the Lord.
Live as children of light.

Brothers and sisters:
Be imitators of God, as beloved children,
  and live in love,
  as Christ loved us and handed himself over for us
  as a sacrificial offering to God for a fragrant aroma.
Immorality or any impurity or greed
  must not even be mentioned among you,
  as is fitting among holy ones,
  no obscenity or silly or suggestive talk, which is out of
    place,
  but instead, thanksgiving.
Be sure of this,
  that no immoral or impure or greedy person, that is, an
    idolater,
  has any inheritance in the Kingdom of Christ and of God.

Let no one deceive you with empty arguments,
    for because of these things
    the wrath of God is coming upon the disobedient.
So do not be associated with them.
For you were once darkness,
    but now you are light in the Lord.
Live as children of light,
    for light produces every kind of goodness and righteous-
        ness and truth.
Try to learn what is pleasing to the Lord.
Take no part in the fruitless works of darkness;
    rather expose them,
    for it is shameful even to mention the things done by
        them in secret;
    but everything exposed by the light becomes visible,
    for everything that becomes visible is light.
Therefore, it says:
    "Awake, O sleeper,
    and arise from the dead,
    and Christ will give you light."

The word of the Lord.

GOSPEL ACCLAMATION   John 8:12

I am the light of the world, says the Lord;
whoever follows me will have the light of life.

GOSPEL

1
                                                    Matthew 22:34-40

✠ **A reading from the holy Gospel according to Matthew**

You shall love the Lord, your God, with all your heart and your neighbor as yourself.

When the Pharisees heard that Jesus had silenced the Sad-
    ducees,
    they gathered together, and one of them,

a scholar of the law, tested him by asking,
   "Teacher, which commandment in the law is the greatest?"
He said to him,
   "You shall love the Lord, your God,
   with all your heart,
   with all your soul,
   and with all your mind.
This is the greatest and the first commandment.
The second is like it:
   You shall love your neighbor as yourself.
The whole law and the prophets depend on these two commandments."

The Gospel of the Lord.

2   John 13:34-35; 15:10-13

✠ **A reading from the holy Gospel according to John**

I give you a new commandment: love one another.

Jesus said to his Apostles:
"I give you a new commandment: love one another.
As I have loved you, so you also should love one another.
This is how all will know that you are my disciples,
   if you have love for one another.

"If you keep my commandments, you will remain in my love,
   just as I have kept my Father's commandments
   and remain in his love.

"I have told you this so that
   my joy might be in you and
   your joy might be complete.
This is my commandment: love one another as I love you.
No one has greater love than this,
   to lay down one's life for one's friends."

The Gospel of the Lord.

SECOND EXAMPLE

Your mind must be renewed

FIRST READING   Isaiah 1:10-18

A reading from the Book of the Prophet Isaiah

Wash yourselves clean; put away your misdeeds from before my eyes.

Hear the word of the LORD,
　　princes of Sodom!
Listen to the instruction of our God,
　　people of Gomorrah!
What care I for the number of your sacrifices?
　　says the LORD.
I have had enough of whole-burnt rams
　　and fat of fatlings;
In the blood of calves, lambs and goats
　　I find no pleasure.

When you come in to visit me,
　　who asks these things of you?
Trample my courts no more!
　　Bring no more worthless offerings;
　　your incense is loathsome to me.
New moon and sabbath, calling of assemblies,
　　octaves with wickedness: these I cannot bear.

Your new moons and festivals I detest;
　　they weigh me down, I tire of the load.

When you spread out your hands,
　　I close my eyes to you;
Though you pray the more,
　　I will not listen.
Your hands are full of blood!
　　Wash yourselves clean!

Put away your misdeeds from before my eyes;
   cease doing evil; learn to do good.
Make justice your aim: redress the wronged,
   hear the orphan's plea, defend the widow.

Come now, let us set things right,
   says the LORD:
Though your sins be like scarlet,
   they may become white as snow;
Though they be crimson red,
   they may become white as wool.

The word of the Lord.

2

RESPONSORIAL PSALM   Psalm 51:3-4, 12-13, 18-19

℟. (19a) A humbled heart is pleasing to God.

Have mercy on me, O God, in your goodness;
   in the greatness of your compassion wipe out my offense.
Thoroughly wash me from my guilt
   and of my sin cleanse me.

   ℟. A humbled heart is pleasing to God.

A clean heart create for me, O God,
   and a steadfast spirit renew within me.
Cast me not out from your presence,
   and your Holy Spirit take not from me.

   ℟. A humbled heart is pleasing to God.

For you are not pleased with sacrifices;
   should I offer a burnt offering, you would not accept it.
My sacrifice, O God, is a contrite spirit;
   a heart contrite and humbled, O God, you will not spurn.

   ℟. A humbled heart is pleasing to God.

SECOND READING   Ephesians 4:23-32

A reading from the Letter of Saint Paul to the Ephesians

Be renewed in the spirit of your minds.

Be renewed in the spirit of your minds, and put on the new self, created in God's way in righteousness and holiness of truth.

Therefore, putting away falsehood, speak the truth, each one to his neighbor, for we are members one of another. Be angry but do not sin; do not let the sun set on your anger, and do not leave room for the Devil. The thief must no longer steal, but rather labor, doing honest work with his own hands, so that he may have something to share with one in need. No foul language should come out of your mouths, but only such as is good for needed edification, that it may impart grace to those who hear. And do not grieve the Holy Spirit of God, with which you were sealed for the day of redemption. All bitterness, fury, anger, shouting, and reviling must be removed from you, along with all malice. And be kind to one another, compassionate, forgiving one another as God has forgiven you in Christ.

The word of the Lord.

GOSPEL ACCLAMATION   Matthew 11:28

Come to me, all you who labor and are burdened,
and I will give you rest, says the Lord.

GOSPEL   Matthew 5:1-12

✠ **A reading from the holy Gospel according to Matthew**

When Jesus saw the crowds, he went up the mountain,
and his disciples came to him.

When Jesus saw the crowds, he went up the mountain,
and after he had sat down, his disciples came to him.
He began to teach them, saying

"Blessed are the poor in spirit,
for theirs is the Kingdom of heaven.
Blessed are they who mourn,
for they will be comforted.
Blessed are the meek,
for they will inherit the land.
Blessed are they who hunger and thirst for righteousness,
for they will be satisfied.
Blessed are the merciful,
for they will be shown mercy.
Blessed are the clean of heart,
for they will see God.
Blessed are the peacemakers,
for they will be called children of God.
Blessed are they who are persecuted for the sake of righteousness,
for theirs is the Kingdom of heaven.
Blessed are you when they insult you and persecute you
and utter every kind of evil against you falsely because
of me.
Rejoice and be glad,
for your reward will be great in heaven.
Thus they persecuted the prophets who were before you."

2

The Gospel of the Lord.

Other optional texts are given in nos. 101-201.

HOMILY

52. The homily which follows is based on the texts of the readings and should lead the penitents to examine their consciences and renew their lives.

EXAMINATION OF CONSCIENCE

53. A period of time may be spent in making an examination of conscience and in arousing true sorrow for sins. The priest, deacon, or another minister may help the faithful by brief statements or a kind of litany, taking into consideration their circumstances, age, etc.

RITE OF RECONCILIATION

GENERAL CONFESSION OF SINS

54. The deacon or another minister invites all to kneel or bow, and to join in saying a general formula for confession (for example, **I confess to almighty God**). Then they stand and say a litany or sing an appropriate song. **The Lord's Prayer** is always added at the end.

FIRST EXAMPLE

Deacon or minister:

My brothers and sisters, confess your sins and pray for each other, that you may be healed.

All say:

I confess to almighty God,
and to you, my brothers and sisters,
that I have sinned through my own fault

They strike their breast:

in my thoughts and in my words,
in what I have done,
and in what I have failed to do;
and I ask blessed Mary, ever virgin,
all the angels and saints,
and you, my brothers and sisters,
to pray for me to the Lord our God.

Deacon or minister:

The Lord is merciful. He makes us clean of heart and leads us out into his freedom when we acknowledge our guilt. Let us ask him to forgive us and bind up the wounds inflicted by our sins.

Give us the grace of true repentance.

   ℟. We pray you, hear us.

Pardon your servants and release them from the debt of sin.

   ℟. We pray you, hear us.

Forgive your children who confess their sins, and restore them to full communion with your Church.

   ℟. We pray you, hear us.

Renew the glory of baptism in those who have lost it by sin.

   ℟. We pray you, hear us.

Welcome them to your altar, and renew their spirit with the hope of eternal glory.

   ℟. We pray you, hear us.

Keep them faithful to your sacraments and loyal in your service.

   ℟. We pray you, hear us.

Renew your love in their hearts, and make them bear witness to it in their daily lives.

   ℟. We pray you, hear us.

Keep them always obedient to your commandments and protect within them your gift of eternal life.

   ℟. We pray you, hear us.

Deacon or minister:

Let us now pray to God our Father in the words Christ gave us, and ask him for his forgiveness and protection from all evil.

All say together:

Our Father . . .

The priest concludes:

Lord,
draw near to your servants
who in the presence of your Church
confess that they are sinners.
Through the ministry of the Church
free them from all sin
so that renewed in spirit
they may give you thankful praise.
We ask this through Christ our Lord.

℞. Amen.

SECOND EXAMPLE

Deacon or minister:

Brothers and sisters, let us call to mind the goodness of God our Father, and acknowledge our sins, so that we may receive his merciful forgiveness.

All say:

I confess to almighty God,
and to you, my brothers and sisters,
that I have sinned through my own fault

They strike their breast:

in my thoughts and in my words,
in what I have done,
and in what I have failed to do;
and I ask blessed Mary, ever virgin,
all the angels and saints,
and you, my brothers and sisters,
to pray for me to the Lord our God.

Deacon or minister:

Christ our Savior is our advocate with the Father: with humble hearts let us ask him to forgive us our sins and cleanse us from every stain.

2

You were sent with good news for the poor and healing for the contrite.

℞. Lord, be merciful to me, a sinner.

OR:

Lord, have mercy.

You came to call sinners, not the just.

℞. Lord, be merciful to me, a sinner.

OR:

Lord, have mercy.

You forgave the many sins of the woman who showed you great love.

℞. Lord, be merciful to me, a sinner.

OR:

Lord, have mercy.

You did not shun the company of outcasts and sinners.

℞. Lord, be merciful to me, a sinner.

OR:
Lord, have mercy.

You carried back to the fold the sheep that had strayed.

℟. Lord, be merciful to me, a sinner.
OR:
Lord, have mercy.

You did not condemn the woman taken in adultery, but sent her away in peace.

℟. Lord, be merciful to me, a sinner.
OR:
Lord, have mercy.

You called Zacchaeus to repentance and a new life.

℟. Lord, be merciful to me, a sinner.
OR:
Lord, have mercy.

You promised Paradise to the repentant thief.

℟. Lord, be merciful to me, a sinner.
OR:
Lord, have mercy.

You are always interceding for us at the right hand of the Father.

℟. Lord, be merciful to me, a sinner.
OR:
Lord, have mercy.

Deacon or minister:

Now, in obedience to Christ himself, let us join in prayer to the Father, asking him to forgive us as we forgive others.

All say together:

Our Father . . .

The priest concludes:

Father, our source of life,
you know our weakness.
May we reach out with joy to grasp your hand
and walk more readily in your ways.
We ask this through Christ our Lord.

℟. Amen.

See page **141** for other examples.

2

INDIVIDUAL CONFESSION AND ABSOLUTION

55. Then the penitents go to the priests designated for individual confession, and confess their sins. Each one receives and accepts a fitting act of satisfaction and is absolved. After hearing the confession and offering suitable counsel, the priest extends his hands over the penitent's head (or at least extends his right hand) and gives him absolution. Everything else which is customary in individual confession is omitted.

God, the Father of mercies,
through the death and resurrection of his Son
has reconciled the world to himself
and sent the Holy Spirit among us
for the forgiveness of sins;
through the ministry of the Church
may God give you pardon and peace,
and I absolve you from your sins
in the name of the Father, and of the Son, ✠
and of the Holy Spirit.

The penitent answers:

℟. Amen.

PROCLAMATION OF PRAISE FOR GOD'S MERCY

56. When the individual confessions have been completed, the other priests stand near the one who is presiding over the celebration. The latter invites all present to offer thanks and encourages them to do good works which will proclaim the grace of repentance in the life of the entire community and each of its members. It is fitting for all to sing a psalm or hymn or to say a litany in acknowledgment of God's power and mercy, for example, the canticle of Mary (Luke 1:46-55), or Psalm 136:1-9, 16, 24-26.

Canticle of Mary   (Luke 1:46-55)

My soul proclaims the greatness of the Lord,
  my spirit rejoices in God my Savior
    for he has looked with favor on his lowly servant.

From this day all generations will call me blessed:
  the Almighty has done great things for me,
    and holy is his Name.

He has mercy on those who fear him
   in every generation.

He has shown the strength of his arm,
   he has scattered the proud in their conceit.

He has cast down the mighty from their thrones,
   and has lifted up the lowly.

He has filled the hungry with good things,
   and the rich he has sent away empty.

He has come to the help of his servant Israel
   for he has remembered his promise of mercy,
   the promise he made to our fathers,
   to Abraham and his children for ever.

2

1   Psalm 136:1-9, 16, 24-26

Give thanks to the LORD, for he is good,
   for his mercy endures forever;
give thanks to the God of gods,
   for his mercy endures forever;
give thanks to the LORD of lords,
   for his mercy endures forever;

Who alone does great wonders,
   for his mercy endures forever;
who made the heavens in wisdom,
   for his mercy endures forever;
who spread out the earth upon the waters,
   for his mercy endures forever;

Who made the great lights,
   for his mercy endures forever;
the sun to rule over the day,
   for his mercy endures forever;
the moon and the stars to rule over the night,
   for his mercy endures forever;

who led his people through the wilderness,
   for his mercy endures forever;

Who freed us from our foes,
   for his mercy endures forever;
who gives food to all flesh,
   for his mercy endures forever;
give thanks to the God of heaven,
   for his mercy endures forever.

2

For other texts, select one from pages **150-164**.

CONCLUDING PRAYER OF THANKSGIVING

57. After the song of praise or the litany, the priest concludes the common prayer:

1

Almighty and merciful God,
how wonderfully you created man
and still more wonderfully remade him.
You do not abandon the sinner
but seek him out with a father's love.
You sent your Son into the world
to destroy sin and death
by his passion,
and to restore life and joy
by his resurrection.
You sent the Holy Spirit into our hearts
to make us your children
and heirs of your kingdom.
You constantly renew our spirit
in the sacrament of your redeeming love,
freeing us from slavery to sin
and transforming us ever more closely

into the likeness of your beloved Son.
We thank you for the wonders of your mercy,
and with heart and hand and voice
we join with the whole Church
in a new song or praise:
Glory to you
through Christ
in the Holy Spirit,
now and for ever.

℟. Amen.

2

All-holy Father,
you have shown us your mercy
and made us a new creation
in the likeness of your Son.
Make us living signs of your love
for the whole world to see.
We ask this through Christ our Lord.

℟. Amen.

3

Father, all-powerful and ever-living God,
we do well always and everywhere to give you thanks.

When you punish us, you show your justice;
when you pardon us, you show your kindness;
yet always your mercy enfolds us.

When you chastise us, you do not wish to condemn us;
when you spare us, you give us time to make amends for
   our sins
through Christ our Lord.

℟. Amen.

4

Lord God,   [208]
creator and ruler of your kingdom of light,
in your great love for this world
you gave up your only Son
for our salvation.
His cross has redeemed us,
his death has given us life,
his resurrection has raised us to glory.
Through him we ask you
to be always present among your family.
Teach us to be reverent in the presence of your glory;
fill our hearts with faith,
our days with good works,
our lives with your love;
may your truth be on our lips
and your wisdom in all our actions,
that we may receive the reward of everlasting life.

We ask this through Christ our Lord.

℞. Amen.

5

Lord Jesus Christ,   [209]
your loving forgiveness knows no limits.
You took our human nature
to give us an example of humility
and to make us faithful in every trial.
May we never lose the gifts you have given us,
but if we fall into sin
lift us up by your gift of repentance,
for you live and reign for ever and ever.

℞. Amen.

6 [210]

Father,
in your love you have brought us
from evil to good and from misery to happiness.
Through your blessings
give the courage of perseverance
to those you have called and justified by faith.
Grant this through Christ our Lord.

℟. Amen.

7

God and Father of us all,
you have forgiven our sins
and sent us your peace.
Help us to forgive each other
and to work together to establish peace in the world.
We ask this through Christ our Lord.

℟. Amen.

CONCLUDING RITE

58. Then the priest blesses all present:

1

May the Lord guide your hearts in the way of his love
and fill you with Christ-like patience. ℟. Amen.

May he give you strength
to walk in newness of life
and to please him in all things. ℟. Amen.

May almighty God bless you,
the Father, and the Son, ✠ and the Holy Spirit. ℟. Amen.

2

And may the blessing of almighty God,
the Father, and the Son, ✠ and the Holy Spirit,
come upon you and remain with you for ever ℟. Amen.

3

May the Father bless us,
for we are his children, born to eternal life. ℟. Amen.

May the Son show us his saving power,
for he died and rose for us. ℟. Amen.

May the Spirit give us his gift of holiness
and lead us by the right path,
for he dwells in our hearts. ℟. Amen.

4

May the Father bless us,
for he has adopted us as his children. ℟. Amen.

May the Son come to help us,
for he has received us as brothers and sisters. ℟. Amen.

May the Spirit be with us,
for he has made us his dwelling place. ℟. Amen.

59. The deacon or other minister or the priest himself dismisses the assembly:

The Lord has freed you from your sins. Go in peace.

All answer:

Thanks be to God.

Any other appropriate form may be used.

CHAPTER III

RITE FOR RECONCILIATION OF SEVERAL PENITENTS WITH GENERAL CONFESSION AND ABSOLUTION

3

OUTLINE

INTRODUCTORY RITES

    Song
    Greeting
    Introduction
    Opening Prayer

CELEBRATION OF THE WORD OF GOD

    First Reading
    Responsorial Psalm
    Second Reading
    Gospel Acclamations
    Gospel
    Homily

GENERAL CONFESSION

    Sign of Penance
    General Confession of Sins
    Litany or Song
    Lord's Prayer

GENERAL ABSOLUTION

PROCLAMATION OF PRAISE AND CONCLUSION

    Song or Hymn
    Blessing
    Dismissal

RITE FOR RECONCILIATION OF SEVERAL PENITENTS WITH GENERAL CONFESSION AND ABSOLUTION

60. For the reconciliation of several penitents with general confession and absolution, in the cases provided for in the law, everything is done as described above for the reconciliation of several penitents with individual absolution, but with the following changes only.

INSTRUCTION

After the homily or as part of the homily, the priest explains to the faithful who wish to receive general absolution that they should be properly disposed. Each one should repent of his sins and resolve to turn away from these sins, to make up for any scandal and harm he may have caused, and to confess individually at the proper time each of the serious sins which cannot now be confessed. Some form of satisfaction should be proposed to all, and each individual may add something if he desires.

GENERAL CONFESSION

61. Then the deacon or other minister or the priest himself invites the penitents who wish to receive absolution to indicate this by some kind of sign. He may say:

1

Will those of you who wish to receive sacramental absolution please kneel and acknowledge that you are sinners.

2

Will those of you who wish to receive sacramental absolution please bow your heads and acknowledge that you are sinners.

Or he may suggest a sign laid down by the episcopal conference.

The penitents say a general formula for confession (for example, I confess to almighty God). A litany or appropriate song may follow, as described above for the reconciliation of several penitents with individual confession and absolution (no. **54**). **The Lord's Prayer** is always added at the end.

GENERAL ABSOLUTION

62. The priest then gives absolution, holding his hands extended over the penitents and saying:

1

God the Father does not wish the sinner to die
but to turn back to him and live.
He loved us first and sent his Son into the world to be its
   Savior.
May he show you his merciful love and give you peace.

R̷. Amen.

Our Lord Jesus Christ was given up to death for our sins,
and rose again for our justification.
He sent the Holy Spirit on his apostles
and gave them power to forgive sins.
Through the ministry entrusted to me
may he deliver you from evil
and fill you with the Holy Spirit.

R̷. Amen.

The Spirit, the Comforter, was given to us for the forgiveness of sins.
In him we approach the Father.
May he cleanse your hearts and clothe you in his glory,
so that you may proclaim the mighty acts of God
who has called you out of darkness into the splendor of
   his light.

R̷. Amen.

And I absolve you from your sins
in the name of the Father, and of the Son, ✝
and of the Holy Spirit.

R̷. Amen.

2

God, the Father of mercies,
through the death and resurrection of his Son
has reconciled the world to himself
and sent the Holy Spirit among us
for the forgiveness of sins;
through the ministry of the Church
may God give you pardon and peace,
and I absolve you from your sins
in the name of the Father, and of the Son, ✠
and of the Holy Spirit.

℟. Amen.

PROCLAMATION OF PRAISE AND CONCLUSION

3

63. The priest invites all to thank God and to acknowledge his mercy. After a suitable song or hymn, he blesses the people and dismisses them, as described above, nos. **58-59**, but without the concluding prayer (no. **57**).

SHORT RITE

64. In case of necessity, the rite for reconciling several penitents with general confession and absolution may be shortened. If possible, there is a brief reading from scripture. After giving the usual instruction (no. **60**) and indicating the act of penance, the priest invites the penitents to make a general confession (for example, **I confess to almighty God**), and gives the absolution with the form which is indicated in no. **62**.

65. In imminent danger of death, it is enough for the priest to use the form of absolution itself. In this case it may be shortened to the following:

**I absolve you from your sins
in the name of the Father, and of the Son, ✠
and of the Holy Spirit.**

℟. Amen.

66. A person who receives general absolution from grave sins is bound to confess each grave sin at his next individual confession.

CHAPTER IV

VARIOUS TEXTS
USED IN THE
CELEBRATION OF RECONCILIATION

VARIOUS TEXTS USED IN THE CELEBRATION OF RECONCILIATION

I. FOR THE RECONCILIATION OF ONE PENITENT

INVITATION TO TRUST IN GOD

67.   (Ezekiel 33:11)

The Lord does not wish the sinner to die
but to turn back to him and live.
Come before him with trust in his mercy.

68.   (Luke 5:32)

May the Lord Jesus welcome you.
He came to call sinners, not the just.
Have confidence in him.

69.

May the grace of the Holy Spirit
fill your heart with light,
that you may confess your sins with loving trust
and come to know that God is merciful.

70.

May the Lord be in your heart
and help you to confess your sins with true sorrow.

71.   (1 John 2:1-2)

If you have sinned, do not lose heart.
We have Jesus Christ to plead for us with the Father:
he is the holy One,
The atonement for our sins
and for the sins of the whole world.

77

Short Readings from Scripture

72.

Let us look on Jesus
who suffered to save us
and rose again for our justification:

Isaiah 53:4-6

Yet it was our infirmities that he bore,
    our sufferings that he endured,
While we thought of him as stricken,
    as one smitten by God and afflicted.
But he was pierced for our offenses,
    crushed for our sins;
Upon him was the chastisement that makes us whole,
    by his stripes we were healed.
We had all gone astray like sheep,
    each following his own way;
But the LORD laid upon him
    the guilt of us all.

73.   Ezekiel 11:19-20

Listen to what the Lord says to us:
I will give them a new heart
    and put a new spirit within them;
    I will remove the stony heart from their bodies,
    and replace it with a natural heart,
    so that they will live according to my statutes,
    and observe and carry out my ordinances;
    thus they shall be my people and I will be their God.

74.   Matthew 6:14-15

Listen to what the Lord says to us:
"If you forgive men their transgressions,
    your heavenly Father will forgive you.

But if you do not forgive men,
　　neither will your Father forgive your transgressions."

75.

Mark 1:14-15

After John had been arrested,
　　Jesus came to Galilee proclaiming the Gospel of God:
　　"This is the time of fulfillment.
The Kingdom of God is at hand.
Repent, and believe in the Gospel."

76.

Luke 6:31-38

Listen to what the Lord says to us:
"Do to others as you would have them do to you.
For if you love those who love you,
　　what credit is that to you?
Even sinners love those who love them.
And if you do good to those who do good to you,
　　what credit is that to you?
Even sinners do the same.
If you lend money to those from whom you expect repayment,
　　what credit is that to you?
Even sinners lend to sinners,
　　and get back the same amount.
But rather, love your enemies and do good to them,
　　and lend expecting nothing back;
　　then your reward will be great
　　and you will be children of the Most High,
　　for he himself is kind to the ungrateful and the wicked.
Be merciful, just as also your Father is merciful.

"Stop judging and you will not be judged.
Stop condemning and you will not be condemned.
Forgive and you will be forgiven.
Give and gifts will be given to you;
　　a good measure, packed together, shaken down, and
　　　overflowing,
　　will be poured into your lap.

For the measure with which you measure
   will in return be measured out to you."

   77.   Luke 15:1-7

The tax collectors and sinners were all drawing near to lis-
      ten to Jesus,
   but the Pharisees and scribes began to complain, saying,
   "This man welcomes sinners and eats with them."
So Jesus addressed this parable to them.
"What man among you having a hundred sheep and losing
      one of them
   would not leave the ninety-nine in the desert
   and go after the lost one until he finds it?
And when he does find it,
   he sets it on his shoulders with great joy
   and, upon his arrival home,
   he calls together his friends and neighbors and says to
      them,
   'Rejoice with me because I have found my lost sheep.'
I tell you, in just the same way
   there will be more joy in heaven over one sinner who re-
      pents
   than over ninety-nine righteous people
   who have no need of repentance."

   78.   John 20:19-23

On the evening of that first day of the week,
   when the doors were locked, where the disciples were,
   for fear of the Jews,
   Jesus came and stood in their midst
   and said to them, "Peace be with you."
When he had said this, he showed them his hands and his side.
The disciples rejoiced when they saw the Lord.
Jesus said to them again, "Peace be with you.
As the Father has sent me, so I send you."

And when he had said this, he breathed on them and said to
　　them,
　　"Receive the Holy Spirit.
Whose sins you forgive are forgiven them,
　　and whose sins you retain are retained."

79.　　　　　　　　　　　　　　　　　　　　Romans 5:8-9

God proves his love for us
　　in that while we were still sinners Christ died for us.
How much more then, since we are now justified by his
　　Blood,
　　will we be saved through him from the wrath.

80.　　　　　　　　　　　　　　　　　　　Ephesians 5:1-2

So be imitators of God, as beloved children, and live in love,
　　as Christ loved us and handed himself over for us
　　as a sacrificial offering to God for a fragrant aroma.

81.　　　　　　　　　　　　　　　　　Colossians 1:12-14

Let us give thanks to the Father,
　　who has made you fit to share
　　in the inheritance of the holy ones in light.
He delivered us from the power of darkness
　　and transferred us to the Kingdom of his beloved Son,
　　in whom we have redemption, the forgiveness of sins.

82.　　　　　　　　　　　　Colossians 3:8 and 5, 9-10, 12-17

Now you must put them all away:
　　anger, fury, malice, slander,
　　and obscene language out of your mouths.
Put to death, then, the parts of you that are earthly:
　　immorality, impurity, passion, evil desire,
　　and the greed that is idolatry.
Stop lying to one another,
　　since you have taken off the old self with its practices
　　and have put on the new self,

which is being renewed, for knowledge,
in the image of its creator.

Put on, as God's chosen ones, holy and beloved,
heartfelt compassion, kindness, humility, gentleness, and
patience,
bearing with one another and forgiving one another,
if one has a grievance against another;
as the Lord has forgiven you, so must you also do.
And over all these put on love,
that is, the bond of perfection.
And let the peace of Christ control your hearts,
the peace into which you were also called in one Body.
And be thankful.
Let the word of Christ dwell in you richly,
as in all wisdom you teach and admonish one another,
singing psalms, hymns, and spiritual songs
with gratitude in your hearts to God.
And whatever you do, in word or in deed,
do everything in the name of the Lord Jesus,
giving thanks to God the Father through him.

83.   1 John 1:6-7, 9

If we say, "We have fellowship with him,"
while we continue to walk in darkness,
we lie and do not act in truth.
But if we walk in the light as he is in the light,
then we have fellowship with one another,
and the Blood of his Son Jesus cleanses us from all sin.
If we acknowledge our sins, he is faithful and just
and will forgive our sins and cleanse us from every wrongdoing.

84. A reading may also be chosen from those given in nos. 101-201
for the reconciliation of several penitents. The priest and penitent
may choose other readings from scripture.

PRAYER OF THE PENITENT

85.   (Psalm 25:6-7)

Remember that your compassion, O LORD,
    and your love are from of old.
In your kindness remember me,
    because of your goodness, O LORD.

86.   (Psalm 51:4-5)

Thoroughly wash me from my guilt
    and of my sin cleanse me.
For I acknowledge my offense,
    and my sin is before me always.

87.   (Luke 15:18; 18:13)

Father, I have sinned [. . .] against you.
I no longer deserve to be called your son.
Be merciful to me a sinner.

88.

Father of mercy,
like the prodigal son
I return to you and say:
"I have sinned against you
and am no longer worthy to be called your son."
Christ Jesus, Savior of the world,
I pray with the repentant thief
to whom you promised paradise:
"Lord, remember me in your kingdom."
Holy Spirit, fountain of love,
I call on you with trust:
"Purify my heart,
and help me to walk as a child of the light."

89.

Lord Jesus,
you opened the eyes of the blind,
healed the sick,
forgave the sinful woman,
and after Peter's denial confirmed him in your love.
Listen to my prayer:
forgive all my sins,
renew your love in my heart,
help me to live in perfect unity with my fellow Christians
that I may proclaim your saving power to all the world.

90.

Lord Jesus,
you chose to be called the friend of sinners.
By your saving death and resurrection
free me from my sins.
May your peace take root in my heart
and bring forth a harvest
of love, holiness, and truth.

91.

Lord Jesus Christ,
you are the Lamb of God;
you take away the sins of the world.
Through the grace of the Holy Spirit
restore me to friendship with your Father,
cleanse me from every stain of sin
in the blood you shed for me,
and raise me to new life
for the glory of your name.

92.

1

Lord God,
in your goodness have mercy on me:

do not look on my sins,
but take away all my guilt.
Create in me a clean heart
and renew within me an upright spirit.

2

Lord Jesus, Son of God, have mercy on me, a sinner.

AFTER THE ABSOLUTION

93. In place of the proclamation of God's praise and the dismissal, the priest may say:

1

May the Passion of our Lord Jesus Christ,
the intercession of the Blessed Virgin Mary
and of all the saints,
whatever good you do and suffering you endure,
heal your sins,
help you to grow in holiness,
and reward you with eternal life.
Go in peace.

2

The Lord has freed you from sin.
May he bring you safely to his kingdom in heaven.
Glory to him for ever.
  ℞. Amen.

3

Blessed are those
whose sins have been forgiven,
whose evil deeds have been forgotten.
Rejoice in the Lord,
and go in peace.

4

Go in peace,
and proclaim to the world
the wonderful works of God,
who has brought you salvation.

II. FOR THE RECONCILIATION OF SEVERAL PENITENTS

GREETING

94.

Grace, mercy, and peace
from God the Father and Jesus Christ his Son
be with you in truth and love.

℟. Amen.

95.

May God open your hearts to his law
and give you peace;
may he answer your prayers
and restore you to his friendship.

℟. Amen.

96.

Grace and peace be with you
from God our Father
and from the Lord Jesus Christ
who laid down his life for our sins.

℟. Glory to him for ever. Amen.

The greetings from the introductory rites of Mass may also be used.

OPENING PRAYERS

97.

Lord,
turn to us in mercy
and forgive us all our sins
that we may serve you in true freedom.
We ask this through Christ our Lord.

℟. Amen.

98.

Lord our God,
you are patient with sinners
and accept our desire to make amends.
We acknowledge our sins
and are resolved to change our lives.
Help us to celebrate this sacrament of your mercy
so that we may reform our lives
and receive from you the gift of everlasting joy.
We ask this through Christ our Lord.

℟. Amen.

99.

Almighty and merciful God,
you have brought us together in the name of your Son
to receive your mercy and grace in our time of need.
Open our eyes to see the evil we have done.
Touch our hearts and convert us to yourself.

Where sin has divided and scattered,
may your love make one again;
where sin has brought weakness,
may your power heal and strengthen;
where sin has brought death,
may your Spirit raise to new life.

Give us a new heart to love you,
so that our lives may reflect the image of your Son.
May the world see the glory of Christ
revealed in your Church,
and come to know
that he is the one whom you have sent,
Jesus Christ, your Son, our Lord.

℟. Amen.

100.

Father of mercies
and God of all consolation,
you do not wish the sinner to die
but to be converted and live.
Come to the aid of your people,
that they may turn from their sins
and live for you alone.
May we be attentive to your word,
confess our sins, receive your forgiveness,
and be always grateful for your loving kindness.
Help us to live the truth in love
and grow into the fullness of Christ, your Son,
who lives and reigns for ever and ever.

℟. Amen.

BIBLICAL READINGS

The following readings are proposed as a help for pastors and others involved in the selection of readings. For diversity, and according to the nature of the group, other readings may be selected.

READINGS FROM THE OLD TESTAMENT

101. Gn 3:1-19

A reading from the Book of Genesis

She took some of its fruit and ate it.

Now the serpent was the most cunning of all
    the animals
    that the Lord God had made.
The serpent asked the woman,
    "Did God really tell you not to eat
    from any of the trees in the garden?"
The woman answered the serpent:
    "We may eat of the fruit of the trees in the
        garden;
    it is only about the fruit of the tree
    in the middle of the garden that God said,
    'You shall not eat it or even touch it, lest
        you die.' "
But the serpent said to the woman:
    "You certainly will not die!
No, God knows well that the moment you
        eat of it
    your eyes will be opened and you will be
        like gods
    who know what is good and what is evil."
The woman saw that the tree was good for
        food,
    pleasing to the eyes, and desirable for
        gaining wisdom.
So she took some of its fruit and ate it;
    and she also gave some to her husband,
        who was with her,
    and he ate it.
Then the eyes of both of them were opened,
    and they realized that they were naked;
    so they sewed fig leaves together
    and made loincloths for themselves.
When they heard the sound of the Lord God
        moving about in the garden
    at the breezy time of the day,
    the man and his wife hid themselves from
        the Lord God
    among the trees of the garden.

The Lord God called to Adam and asked
        him, "Where are you?"
He answered, "I heard you in the garden;
    but I was afraid, because I was naked,
    so I hid myself."
Then he asked, "Who told you that you
        were naked?
You have eaten, then,
    from the tree of which I had forbidden
        you to eat!"
The man replied, "The woman whom you
        put here with me—
    she gave me fruit from the tree, and so I
        ate it."
The Lord God then asked the woman,
    "Why did you do such a thing?"
The woman answered, "The serpent tricked
        me into it, so I ate it."

Then the Lord God said to the serpent:
    "Because you have done this, you shall
        be banned
    from all the animals
    and from all the wild creatures;
On your belly shall you crawl,
    and dirt shall you eat
    all the days of your life.
I will put enmity between you and the
        woman,
    and between your offspring and hers;
He will strike at your head,
    while you strike at his heel."

To the woman he said:
    "I will intensify the pangs of your child-
        bearing;
    in pain shall you bring forth children.
Yet your urge shall be for your husband,
    and he shall be your master."

To the man he said: "Because you listened
        to your wife
    and ate from the tree of which I had for-
        bidden you to eat,

"Cursed be the ground because of you!
  In toil shall you eat its yield
  all the days of your life.
Thorns and thistles shall it bring forth to
    you,
  as you eat of the plants of the field.
By the sweat of your face
  shall you get bread to eat,
Until you return to the ground,
  from which you were taken;
For you are dirt,
  and to dirt you shall return."

  The word of the Lord.

---

102. Gn 4:1-15

A reading from the Book of Genesis

Cain attacked his brother Abel and killed him.

The man had relations with his wife Eve,
  and she conceived and bore Cain, saying,
  "I have produced a man with the help of
    the LORD."
Next she bore his brother Abel.
Abel became a keeper of flocks, and Cain a
    tiller of the soil.
In the course of time Cain brought an offer-
    ing to the LORD
  from the fruit of the soil,
  while Abel, for his part,
  brought one of the best firstlings of his
    flock.
The LORD looked with favor on Abel and his
    offering,
  but on Cain and his offering he did not.
Cain greatly resented this and was crest-
    fallen.
So the LORD said to Cain:
  "Why are you so resentful and crest-
    fallen.
If you do well, you can hold up your head;
  but if not, sin is a demon lurking at the
    door:
  his urge is toward you, yet you can be his
    master."
Cain said to his brother Abel, "Let us go out
    in the field."
When they were in the field,
  Cain attacked his brother Abel and killed
    him.

Then the LORD asked Cain, "Where is your
    brother Abel?"
He answered, "I do not know.
Am I my brother's keeper?"
The LORD then said: "What have you done!
Listen: your brother's blood cries out to me
    from the soil!
Therefore you shall be banned from the soil
  that opened its mouth to receive
  your brother's blood from your hand.
If you till the soil, it shall no longer give you
    its produce.
You shall become a restless wanderer on
    the earth."
Cain said to the LORD: "My punishment is
    too great to bear.
Since you have now banished me from the
    soil,
  and I must avoid your presence
  and become a restless wanderer on the
    earth,
  anyone may kill me at sight."
"Not so!" the LORD said to him.
"If anyone kills Cain, Cain shall be avenged
    sevenfold."
So the LORD put a mark on Cain, lest anyone
    should kill him at sight.

  The word of the Lord.

---

103. Gn 18:17-33

A reading from the Book of Genesis

For the sake of those ten, I will not destroy it.

The LORD reflected: "Shall I hide from Abra-
    ham what I am about to do,
  now that he is to become a great and pop-
    ulous nation,
  and all the nations of the earth are to find
    blessing in him?
Indeed, I have singled him out
  that he may direct his children and his
    household after him
  to keep the way of the LORD
  by doing what is right and just,
  so that the LORD may carry into effect for
    Abraham
  the promises he made about him."
Then the LORD said:
  "The outcry against Sodom and Gomor-
    rah is so great,

and their sin so grave,
that I must go down and see whether or
not their actions
fully correspond to the cry against them
that comes to me.
I mean to find out.”

While the two men walked on farther toward Sodom,
the LORD remained standing before Abraham.
Then Abraham drew nearer to him and said:
“Will you sweep away the innocent with
the guilty?
Suppose there were fifty innocent people in
the city;
would you wipe out the place, rather than
spare it
for the sake of the fifty innocent people
within it?
Far be it from you to do such a thing,
to make the innocent die with the guilty,
so that the innocent and the guilty would
be treated alike!
Should not the judge of all the world act
with justice?”
The LORD replied,
“If I find fifty innocent people in the city
of Sodom,
I will spare the whole place for their
sake.”
Abraham spoke up again:
“See how I am presuming to speak to my
Lord,
though I am but dust and ashes!
What if there are five less than fifty inno-
cent people?
Will you destroy the whole city because of
those five?”
He answered, “I will not destroy it if I find
forty-five there.”
But Abraham persisted, saying, “What if
only forty are found there?”
He replied, “I will forbear doing it for the
sake of forty.”
Then Abraham said, “Let not my Lord grow
impatient if I go on.
What if only thirty are found there?”
He replied, “I will forbear doing it if I can
find but thirty there.”
Still Abraham went on,

“Since I have thus dared to speak to my
Lord,
what if there are no more than twenty?”
He answered, “I will not destroy it for the
sake of the twenty.”
But he still persisted:
“Please, let not my Lord grow angry if I
speak up this last time.
What if there are at least ten there?”
He replied, “For the sake of those ten, I will
not destroy it.”

The LORD departed as soon as he had finished speaking with Abraham,
and Abraham returned home.

The word of the Lord.

---

104. Ex 17:1-7

A reading from the Book of Exodus

They tested the LORD, saying,
“Is the LORD in our midst or not?”

From the desert of Sin the whole congregation of the children of Israel
journeyed by stages, as the LORD directed,
and encamped at Rephidim.

There was no water for the people to drink.
They quarreled, therefore, with Moses and
said,
“Give us water to drink.”
Moses replied, “Why do you quarrel with
me?
Why do you put the LORD to a test?”
[. . .] Then, in their thirst for water,
the people grumbled against Moses,
saying, “Why did you ever make us leave
Egypt?
Was it just to have us die here of thirst
with our children and our livestock?”
So Moses cried out to the LORD,
“What shall I do with this people?
A little more and they will stone me!”
The LORD answered Moses,
“Go over there in front of the people,
along with some of the elders of Israel,
holding in your hand, as you go,
the staff with which you struck the river.
I will be standing there in front of you on
the rock in Horeb.

Strike the rock, and the water will flow from
  it
  for the people to drink."
This Moses did, in the presence of the elders
  of Israel.
The place was called Massah and Meribah,
  because the children of Israel quarreled
  there
  and tested the LORD, saying,
  "Is the LORD in our midst or not?"

> The word of the Lord.

---

105. Ex 20:1-21

A reading from the Book of Exodus

I, the LORD, am your God. You shall not have other gods.

God delivered all these commandments:

"I, the LORD, am your God,
  who brought you out of the land of Egypt,
  that place of slavery.
You shall not have other gods besides me.
You shall not carve idols for yourselves
  in the shape of anything in the sky above
  or on the earth below or in the waters be-
  neath the earth;
  you shall not bow down before them or
  worship them.
For I, the LORD, your God, am a jealous God,
  inflicting punishment for their fathers'
  wickedness
  on the children of those who hate me,
  down to the third and fourth generation;
  but bestowing mercy down to the thou-
  sandth generation
  on the children of those who love me and
  keep my commandments.
"You shall not take the name of the LORD,
  your God, in vain.
For the LORD will not leave unpunished
  him who takes his name in vain.

"Remember to keep holy the sabbath day.
Six days you may labor and do all your
  work,
  but the seventh day is the sabbath of the
  LORD, your God.
No work may be done then either by you, or
  your son or daughter,
  or your male or female slave, or your beast,
  or by the alien who lives with you.

In six days the LORD made the heavens and
  the earth,
  the sea and all that is in them;
  but on the seventh day he rested.
That is why the LORD has blessed the sabbath day and made it holy.
"Honor your father and your mother,
  that you may have a long life in the land
  which the LORD, your God, is giving you.

"You shall not kill.

"You shall not commit adultery.

"You shall not steal.

"You shall not bear false witness against
  your neighbor.

"You shall not covet your neighbor's house.
You shall not covet your neighbor's wife,
  nor his male or female slave, nor his ox or
  ass
  nor anything else that belongs to him."

When the people witnessed the thunder and
  lightning,
  the trumpet blast and the mountain smok-
  ing,
  they all feared and trembled.
So they took up a position much farther
  away
  and said to Moses,
  "You speak to us, and we will listen;
  but let not God speak to us, or we shall
  die."
Moses answered the people,
  "Do not be afraid,
  for God has come to you only to test you
  and put his fear upon you,
  lest you should sin."
Still the people remained at a distance,
  while Moses approached the cloud where
  God was.

> The word of the Lord.

---

106. Dt 6:4-9

A reading from the Book of Deuteronomy

Love the LORD, your God, with all your heart.

In those days
Moses said to the people:

"Hear, O Israel! The LORD is our God, the LORD alone!

Therefore, you shall love the LORD, your God,
  with all your heart,
  and with all your soul,
  and with all your strength.

Take to heart these words which I enjoin on you today.

Drill them into your children.

Speak of them at home and abroad, whether you are busy or at rest.

Bind them at your wrist as a sign
  and let them be as a pendant on your forehead.

Write them on the doorposts of your houses and on your gates."

The word of the Lord.

---

107. Dt 9:7-19

A reading from the Book of Deuteronomy

Your people have become depraved; they have already turned aside from the way I pointed out to them.

In those days,
  Moses said to the people:
  "Bear in mind and do not forget
  how you angered the LORD, your God, in the desert.

From the day you left the land of Egypt
  until you arrived in this place,
  you have been rebellious toward the LORD.

At Horeb you so provoked the LORD
  that he was angry enough to destroy you,
  when I had gone up the mountain to receive
  the stone tablets of the covenant
  which the LORD made with you.

Meanwhile I stayed on the mountain forty days and forty nights
  without eating or drinking,
  till the LORD gave me the two tablets of stone
  inscribed, by God's own finger, with a copy of all the words
  that the LORD spoke to you on the mountain

from the midst of the fire on the day of the assembly.

Then, at the end of the forty days and forty nights,
  when the LORD had given me the two stone tablets of the covenant, he said to me,
  'Go down from here now, quickly,
  for your people whom you have brought out of Egypt
  have become depraved;
  they have already turned aside from the way I pointed out to them
  and have made for themselves a molten idol.

I have seen now how stiff-necked this people is,' the LORD said to me.

'Let me be, that I may destroy them
  and blot out their name from under the heavens.

I will then make of you a nation mightier and greater than they.'

"When I had come down again from the blazing, fiery mountain,
  with the two tablets of the covenant in both my hands,
  I saw how you had sinned against the LORD, your God:
  you had already turned aside from the way
  which the LORD had pointed out to you
  by making for yourselves a molten calf!

Raising the two tablets with both hands

I threw them from me and broke them before your eyes.

Then, as before, I lay prostrate before the LORD
  for forty days and forty nights without eating or drinking,
  because of all the sin you had committed in the sight of the LORD
  and the evil you had done to provoke him.

For I dreaded the fierce anger of the LORD against you:
  his wrath would destroy you.

Yet once again the LORD listened to me."

The word of the Lord.

---

108. Dt 30:15-20

A reading from the Book of Deuteronomy

Today I have set before you life and prosperity, death and doom.

Moses said to the people:
  "Today I have set before you
  life and prosperity, death and doom.
If you obey the commandments of the LORD,
    your God,
  which I enjoin on you today,
  loving him, and walking in his ways,
  and keeping his commandments, statutes
    and decrees,
  you will live and grow numerous,
  and the LORD, your God,
  will bless you in the land you are entering
    to occupy.
If, however, you turn away your hearts and
    will not listen,
  but are led astray and adore and serve
    other gods,
  I tell you now that you will certainly
    perish;
  you will not have a long life
  on the land that you are crossing the Jordan to enter and occupy.
I call heaven and earth today to witness
    against you:
  I have set before you life and death,
  the blessing and the curse.
Choose life, then,
  that you and your descendants may live,
  by loving the LORD, your God,
  heeding his voice, and holding fast to him.
For that will mean life for you,
  a long life for you to live on the land that
    the LORD swore
  he would give to your fathers Abraham,
    Isaac and Jacob."

The word of the Lord.

---

109. 2 Sm 12:1-9, 13

A reading from the second Book of Samuel

David said to Nathan, "I have sinned against the LORD." Nathan answered David: "The LORD on his part has forgiven your sin: you shall not die."

In those days, the LORD sent Nathan to
    David, and when he came to him,
  he said: "Judge this case for me!
In a certain town there were two men, one
    rich, the other poor.
The rich man had flocks and herds in great
    numbers.
But the poor man had nothing at all
  except one little ewe lamb that he had
    bought.
He nourished her, and she grew up with him
    and his children.
She shared the little food he had
  and drank from his cup and slept in his
    bosom.
She was like a daughter to him.
Now, the rich man received a visitor,
  but he would not take from his own flocks
    and herds
  to prepare a meal for the wayfarer who
    had come to him.
Instead he took the poor man's ewe lamb
  and made a meal of it for his visitor."
David grew very angry with that man and
    said to Nathan:
  "As the LORD lives, the man who has done
    this merits death!
He shall restore the ewe lamb fourfold
  because he has done this and has had no
    pity."
Then Nathan said to David: "You are the
    man!
Thus says the LORD God of Israel:
  'I anointed you king of Israel.
  I rescued you from the hand of Saul.
I gave you your lord's house and your lord's
    wives for your own.
I gave you the house of Israel and of Judah.
And if this were not enough,
  I could count up for you still more.
Why have you spurned the LORD
  and done evil in his sight?

You have cut down Uriah the Hittite with
the sword;
you took his wife as your own,
and him you killed with the sword of the
Ammonites.
Then David said to Nathan, "I have sinned
against the LORD."
Nathan answered David:
"The LORD on his part has forgiven your
sin: you shall not die."

The word of the Lord.

---

110. Neh 9:1-20

A reading from the Book of Nehemiah

*The children of Israel gathered together
fasting and confessed their sins.*

On the twenty-fourth day of this month,
the children of Israel gathered together
fasting and in sackcloth,
their heads covered with dust.
Those descended from the children of Israel
separated themselves
from all who were of foreign extraction,
then stood forward and confessed their sins
and the guilty deeds of their fathers.
When they had taken their places,
they read from the book of the law of the
LORD their God,
for a fourth part of the day,
and during another fourth part they made
their confession
and prostrated themselves before the
LORD their God.
Standing on the platform of the Levites
were Jeshua, Binnui, Kadmiel, Shebaniah,
Bunni, Sherebiah, Bani, and Chenani,
who cried out to the LORD their God, with
a loud voice.
The Levites Jeshua, Kadmiel, Bani, Hashab-
neiah, Sherebiah, Hodiah, Shebaniah,
and Pethahiah said,

"Arise, bless the LORD, your God,
from eternity to eternity!"

The children of Israel answered with the
blessing,

"Blessed is your glorious name,
and exalted above all blessing and
praise."

Then Ezra said: "It is you, O LORD,
you are the only one;
you made the heavens, the highest heavens and all their host,
the earth and all that is upon it,
the seas and all that is in them.
To all of them you give life,
and the heavenly hosts bow down before
you.
"You, O LORD, are the God who chose
Abram,
who brought him out from Ur of the
Chaldees,
and named him Abraham.
When you had found his heart faithful in
your sight,
you made the covenant with him to give to
him and his posterity
the land of the Canaanites, Hittites, Amo-
rites, Perizzites, Jebusites, and Gir-
gashites.
These promises of yours you fulfilled, for
you are just.
"You saw the affliction of our fathers in
Egypt,
you heard their cry by the Red Sea;
You worked signs and wonders against
Pharaoh,
against all his servants and the people of
his land,
Because you knew of their insolence toward
them;
thus you made for yourself a name even to
this day.
The sea you divided before them,
on dry ground they passed through the
midst of the sea;
Their pursuers you hurled into the depths,
like a stone into the mighty waters.
With a column of cloud you led them by day,
and by night with a column of fire,
To light the way of their journey,
the way in which they must travel.
On Mount Sinai you came down,
you spoke with them from heaven;
You gave them just ordinances, firm laws,
good statutes, and commandments;
Your holy sabbath you made known to
them, commandments, statutes, and law
you prescribed for them,
by the hand of Moses your servant.

Food from heaven you gave them in their
  hunger,
    water from a rock you sent them in their
    thirst.
You bade them enter and occupy the land
    which you had sworn with upraised hand
    to give them.

"But they, our fathers, proved to be insolent;
    they held their necks stiff
    and would not obey your commandments.
They refused to obey and no longer remembered
    the miracles you had worked for them.
They stiffened their necks and turned their
    heads
    to return to their slavery in Egypt.
But you are a God of pardons,
    gracious and compassionate, slow to
    anger and rich in mercy;
    you did not forsake them.
Though they made for themselves a molten
    calf, and proclaimed,
    'Here is your God who brought you up out
    of Egypt,'
    and were guilty of great effronteries,
    yet in your great mercy you did not forsake them in the desert.
The column of cloud did not cease to lead
    them by day on their journey,
    nor did the column of fire by night cease
    to light for them
    the way by which they were to travel.

"Your good spirit you bestowed on them,
    to give them understanding;
    your manna you did not withhold from
    their mouths,
    and you gave them water in their thirst."
        The word of the Lord.

---

111. Wis 1:1-16

A reading from the Book of Wisdom

*Love justice because into a soul that plots evil wisdom
enters not, nor dwells she in a body under debt of sin.*

Love justice, you who judge the earth;
    think of the LORD in goodness,
    and seek him in integrity of heart;
Because he is found by those who test him
    not,

and he manifests himself to those who
    do not disbelieve him.
For perverse counsels separate a man from
    God,
    and his power, put to the proof, rebukes
    the foolhardy;
Because into a soul that plots evil wisdom
    enters not,
    nor dwells she in a body under debt of sin.
For the holy spirit of discipline flees deceit
    and withdraws from senseless counsels;
    and when injustice occurs it is rebuked.
For wisdom is a kindly spirit,
    yet she acquits not the blasphemer of his
    guilty lips;
Because God is the witness of his inmost
    self
    and the sure observer of his heart
    and the listener to his tongue.
For the spirit of the LORD fills the world,
    is all-embracing, and knows what man
    says.
Therefore no one who utters wicked things
    can go unnoticed,
    nor will chastising condemnation pass
    him by.
For the devices of the wicked man shall be
    scrutinized,
    and the sound of his words shall reach the
    LORD,
    for the chastisement of his transgressions;
Because a jealous ear hearkens to everything,
    and discordant grumblings are no secret.
Therefore guard against profitless grumbling,
    and from calumny withhold your tongues;
For a stealthy utterance does not go unpunished,
    and a lying mouth slays the soul.
Court not death by your erring way of life,
    nor draw to yourselves destruction by the
    works of your hands.
Because God did not make death,
    nor does he rejoice in the destruction of
    the living.
For he fashioned all things that they might
    have being;
    and the creatures of the world are wholesome,

And there is not a destructive drug among them
> nor any domain of the nether world on earth,

For justice is undying.

It was the wicked who with hands and words invited death,
> considered it a friend, and pined for it,
> and made a covenant with it,

Because they deserve to be in its possession.

> The word of the Lord.

---

112. Wis 5:1-16

A reading from the Book of Wisdom

The hope of the wicked is like thistledown borne on the wind. But the just live forever.

Then shall the just one with great assurance confront
> his oppressors who set at nought his labors.

Seeing this, they shall be shaken with dreadful fear,
> and amazed at the unlooked-for salvation.

They shall say among themselves, rueful
> and groaning through anguish of spirit:

"This is he whom once we held as a laughingstock
> and as a type for mockery, fools that we were!

His life we accounted madness,
> and his death dishonored.

See how he is accounted among the sons of God;
> how his lot is with the saints!

We, then, have strayed from the way of truth,
> and the light of justice did not shine for us, and the sun did not rise for us.

We had our fill of the ways of mischief and of ruin;
> we journeyed through impassable deserts, but the way of the LORD we knew not.

What did our pride avail us?
> What have wealth and its boastfulness afforded us?

All of them passed like a shadow
> and like a fleeting rumor;

Like a ship traversing the heaving water,
> of which, when it has passed, no trace can be found,
> no path of its keel in the waves.

Or like a bird flying through the air;
> no evidence of its course is to be found—

But the fluid air, lashed by the beat of pinions,
> and cleft by the rushing force

Of speeding wings, is traversed:
> and afterward no mark of passage can be found in it.

Or as, when an arrow has been shot at a mark,
> the parted air straightway flows together again
> so that none discerns the way it went through—

Even so we, once born, abruptly came to nought
> and held no sign of virtue to display,
> but were consumed in our wickedness."

Yes, the hope of the wicked is like thistledown borne on the wind,
> and like fine, tempest-driven foam;

Like smoke scattered by the wind,
> and like the passing memory of the nomad camping for a single day.

But the just live forever,
> and in the LORD is their recompense,
> and the thought of them is with the Most High.

Therefore shall they receive the splendid crown,
> the beauteous diadem, from the hand of the LORD—

For he shall shelter them with his right hand,
> and protect them with his arm.

> The word of the Lord.

---

113. Sir 28:1-7

A reading from the Book of Sirach

Forgive your neighbor's injustice; then when you pray,
your own sins will be forgiven.

The vengeful will suffer the LORD's vengeance,
  for he remembers their sins in detail.
Forgive your neighbor's injustice;
  then when you pray, your own sins will be
  forgiven.
Should a man nourish anger against his fellows
  and expect healing from the LORD?
Should a man refuse mercy to his fellows,
  yet seek pardon for his own sins?
If he who is but flesh cherishes wrath,
  who will forgive his sins?
Remember your last days, set enmity aside;
  remember death and decay, and cease
  from sin!
Think of the commandments, hate not your
  neighbor;
  of the Most High's covenant, and overlook
  faults.

The word of the Lord.

The whole head is sick,
  the whole heart faint.
From the sole of the foot to the head
  there is no sound spot:
Wound and welt and gaping gash,
  not drained, or bandaged,
  or eased with salve.

When you spread out your hands,
  I close my eyes to you;
Though you pray the more,
  I will not listen.
Your hands are full of blood!
  Wash yourselves clean!
Put away your misdeeds from before my
  eyes;
  cease doing evil; learn to do good.
Make justice your aim: redress the wronged,
  hear the orphan's plea, defend the widow.

Come now, let us set things right,
  says the LORD:
Though your sins be like scarlet,
  they may become white as snow;
Though they be crimson red,
  they may become white as wool.

The word of the Lord.

114. Is 1:2-6, 15-18

A reading from the Book of the
Prophet Isaiah

Sons have I raised and reared,
but they have disowned me!

Hear, O heavens, and listen, O earth,
  for the LORD speaks:
Sons have I raised and reared,
  but they have disowned me!
An ox knows its owner,
  and an ass, its master's manger;
But Israel does not know,
  my people has not understood.
Ah! sinful nation, people laden with wickedness,
  evil race, corrupt children!
They have forsaken the LORD,
  spurned the Holy One of Israel,
  apostatized.
Where would you yet be struck,
  you that rebel again and again?

115. Is 5:1-7

A reading from the Book of the
Prophet Isaiah

My friend had a vineyard.
He looked for the crop of grapes, but what it yielded was
wild grapes.

Let me now sing of my friend,
  my friend's song concerning his vineyard.
My friend had a vineyard
  on a fertile hillside;
He spaded it, cleared it of stones,
  and planted the choicest vines;
Within it he built a watchtower,
  and hewed out a wine press.
Then he looked for the crop of grapes,
  but what it yielded was wild grapes.
Now, inhabitants of Jerusalem and people
  of Judah,
  judge between me and my vineyard:

What more was there to do for my vineyard
   that I had not done?
Why, when I looked for the crop of grapes,
   did it bring forth wild grapes?
Now, I will let you know
   what I mean to do with my vineyard:
Take away its hedge, give it to grazing,
   break through its wall, let it be trampled!
Yes, I will make it a ruin:
   it shall not be pruned or hoed,
   but overgrown with thorns and briers;
I will command the clouds
   not to send rain upon it.
The vineyard of the LORD of hosts is the
   house of Israel,
   and the people of Judah are his cher-
   ished plant;
He looked for judgment, but see, blood-
   shed!
   for justice, but hark, the outcry!

     The word of the Lord.

---

116. Is 43:22-28

A reading from the Book of the Prophet Isaiah

It is I, I, who wipe out, for my own sake, your offenses.

Thus says the Lord:
Yet you did not call upon me, O Jacob,
   for you grew weary of me, O Israel.
You did not bring me sheep for your burnt
   offerings,
   nor honor me with your sacrifices.
I did not exact from you the service of offerings,
   nor weary you for frankincense.
You did not buy me sweet cane for money,
   nor fill me with the fat of your sacrifices;
Instead, you burdened me with your sins,
   and wearied me with your crimes.
It is I, I, who wipe out,
   for my own sake, your offenses;
   your sins I remember no more.
Would you have me remember, have us
   come to trial?
   Speak up, prove your innocence!
Your first father sinned;
   your spokesmen rebelled against me

Till I repudiated the holy gates,
   put Jacob under the ban,
   and exposed Israel to scorn.

     The word of the Lord.

---

117. Is 53:1-12

A reading from the Book of the Prophet Isaiah

The LORD laid upon him the guilt of us all.

Who would believe what we have heard?
   To whom has the arm of the LORD been
   revealed?
He grew up like a sapling before him,
   like a shoot from the parched earth;
There was in him no stately bearing to make
   us look at him,
   nor appearance that would attract us to
   him.
He was spurned and avoided by people,
   a man of suffering, accustomed to infirmity,
One of those from whom people hide their
   faces,
   spurned, and we held him in no esteem.

Yet it was our infirmities that he bore,
   our sufferings that he endured,
While we thought of him as stricken,
   as one smitten by God and afflicted.
But he was pierced for our offenses,
   crushed for our sins;
Upon him was the chastisement that makes
   us whole,
   by his stripes we were healed.
We had all gone astray like sheep,
   each following his own way;
But the LORD laid upon him
   the guilt of us all.

Though he was harshly treated, he submit-
   ted
   and opened not his mouth;
Like a lamb led to the slaughter
   or a sheep before the shearers,
   he was silent and opened not his mouth.
Oppressed and condemned, he was taken
   away,
   and who would have thought any more of
   his destiny?

When he was cut off from the land of the
　　living,
　　and smitten for the sin of his people,
A grave was assigned him among the
　　wicked
　　and a burial place with evildoers,
Though he had done no wrong
　　nor spoken any falsehood.
But the Lord was pleased
　　to crush him in infirmity.

If he gives his life as an offering for sin,
　　he shall see his descendants in a long life,
　　and the will of the Lord shall be accom-
　　plished through him.

Because of his affliction
　　he shall see the light in fullness of days;
Through his suffering, my servant shall jus-
　　tify many,
　　and their guilt he shall bear.
Therefore I will give him his portion among
　　the great,
　　and he shall divide the spoils with the
　　mighty,
Because he surrendered himself to death
　　and was counted among the wicked;
And he shall take away the sins of many,
　　and win pardon for their offenses.

The word of the Lord.

---

118. Is 55:1-11

A reading from the Book of the Prophet Isaiah

Let the scoundrel forsake his way, and the wicked man his thoughts; let him turn to the Lord for mercy; to our God, who is generous in forgiving.

All you who are thirsty,
　　come to the water!
You who have no money,
　　come, receive grain and eat;
Come, without paying and without cost,
　　drink wine and milk!
Why spend your money for what is not
　　bread,
　　your wages for what fails to satisfy?
Heed me, and you shall eat well,
　　you shall delight in rich fare.
Come to me heedfully,
　　listen, that you may have life.

I will renew with you the everlasting cove-
　　nant,
　　the benefits assured to David.
As I made him a witness to the peoples,
　　a leader and commander of nations,
So shall you summon a nation you knew not,
　　and nations that knew you not shall run to
　　you,
Because of the Lord, your God,
　　the Holy One of Israel, who has glorified
　　you.

Seek the Lord while he may be found,
　　call him while he is near.
Let the scoundrel forsake his way,
　　and the wicked man his thoughts;
Let him turn to the Lord for mercy;
　　to our God, who is generous in forgiving.
For my thoughts are not your thoughts,
　　nor are your ways my ways, says the
　　Lord.
As high as the heavens are above the earth,
　　so high are my ways above your ways
　　and my thoughts above your thoughts.

For just as from the heavens
　　the rain and snow come down
And do not return there
　　till they have watered the earth,
　　making it fertile and fruitful,
Giving seed to the one who sows
　　and bread to the one who eats,
So shall my word be
　　that goes forth from my mouth;
My word shall not return to me void,
　　but shall do my will,
　　achieving the end for which I sent it.

The word of the Lord.

---

119. Is 58:1-11

A reading from the Book of the Prophet Isaiah

Then light shall rise for you in the darkness, and the gloom shall become for you like midday.

Thus says the Lord:
Cry out full-throated and unsparingly,
　　lift up your voice like a trumpet blast;
Tell my people their wickedness,
　　and the house of Jacob their sins.
They seek me day after day,
　　and desire to know my ways,

Like a nation that has done what is just
  and not abandoned the law of their
  God;
They ask me to declare what is due them,
  pleased to gain access to God.
"Why do we fast, and you do not see it?
  afflict ourselves, and you take no note of
  it?"

Lo, on your fast day you carry out your own
  pursuits,
  and drive all your laborers.
Yes, your fast ends in quarreling and fight-
  ing,
  striking with wicked claw.
Would that today you might fast
  so as to make your voice heard on high!
Is this the manner of fasting I wish,
  of keeping a day of penance:
That a man bow his head like a reed
  and lie in sackcloth and ashes?
Do you call this a fast,
  a day acceptable to the LORD?
This, rather, is the fasting that I wish:
  releasing those bound unjustly,
  untying the thongs of the yoke;
Setting free the oppressed,
  breaking every yoke;
Sharing your bread with the hungry,
  sheltering the oppressed and the home-
  less;
Clothing the naked when you see them,
  and not turning your back on your own.
Then your light shall break forth like the
  dawn,
  and your wound shall quickly be healed;
Your vindication shall go before you,
  and the glory of the LORD shall be your
  rear guard.
Then you shall call, and the LORD will answer,
  you shall cry for help, and he will say:
  Here I am!
If you remove from your midst oppression,
  false accusation and malicious speech;
If you bestow your bread on the hungry
  and satisfy the afflicted;
Then light shall rise for you in the darkness,
  and the gloom shall become for you like
  midday;

Then the LORD will guide you always
  and give you plenty even on the parched
  land.
He will renew your strength,
  and you shall be like a watered garden,
  like a spring whose water never fails.
  for the mouth of the LORD has spoken.

The word of the Lord.

---

120. Is 59:1-4, 9-15

A reading from the Book of the Prophet Isaiah

It is your crimes that separate you from your God.

Lo, the hand of the LORD is not too short to
  save,
  nor his ear too dull to hear.
Rather, it is your crimes
  that separate you from your God,
It is your sins that make him hide his face
  so that he will not hear you.
For your hands are stained with blood,
  your fingers with guilt;
Your lips speak falsehood,
  and your tongue utters deceit.
No one brings suit justly,
  no one pleads truthfully;
They trust in emptiness and tell lies;
  they conceive mischief and bring forth
  malice.

That is why right is far from us
  and justice does not reach us.
We look for light, and lo, darkness;
  for brightness, but we walk in gloom!
Like blind men we grope along the wall,
  like people without eyes we feel our way.
We stumble at midday as at dusk,
  in Stygian darkness, like the dead.
We all growl like bears,
  like doves we moan without ceasing.
We look for right, but it is not there;
  for salvation, and it is far from us.
For our offenses before you are many,
  our sins bear witness against us.
Yes, our offenses are present to us,
  and our crimes we know:
Transgressing, and denying the LORD,
  turning back from following our God,

Threatening outrage, and apostasy,
    uttering words of falsehood the heart has
      conceived.
Right is repelled,
    and justice stands far off;
For truth stumbles in the public square,
    uprightness cannot enter.
Honesty is lacking,
    and the man who turns from evil is de-
      spoiled.
The LORD saw this, and was aggrieved
    that right did not exist.

The word of the Lord.

---

121. Jer 2:1-13

A reading from the Book of the Prophet Jeremiah

Two evils have my people done: they have forsaken me,
the source of living waters;
They have dug themselves cisterns, broken cisterns,
that hold no water.

This word of the LORD came to me:
Go, cry out this message for Jerusalem to
    hear!
I remember the devotion of your youth,
    how you loved me as a bride,
Following me in the desert,
    in a land unsown.
Sacred to the LORD was Israel,
    the first fruits of his harvest;
Should anyone presume to partake of them,
    evil would befall him, says the LORD.

Listen to the word of the LORD, O house of
    Jacob!
    All you clans of the house of Israel,
    thus says the LORD:
What fault did your fathers find in me
    that they withdrew from me,
Went after empty idols,
    and became empty themselves?
They did not ask, "Where is the LORD
    who brought us up from the land of Egypt,
Who led us through the desert,
    through a land of wastes and gullies,
Through a land of drought and darkness,
    through a land which no one crosses,
    where no man dwells?"
When I brought you into the garden land
    to eat its goodly fruits,

You entered and defiled my land,
    you made my heritage loathsome.
The priests asked not,
    "Where is the LORD?"
Those who dealt with the law knew me not:
    the shepherds rebelled against me.
The prophets prophesied by Baal,
    and went after useless idols.
Therefore will I yet accuse you, says the
    LORD,
    and even your children's children I will
    accuse.
Pass over to the coast of the Kittim and see,
    send to Kedar and carefully inquire:
    Where has the like of this been done?
Does any other nation change its gods?—
    yet they are not gods at all!
But my people have changed their glory
    for useless things.
Be amazed at this, O heavens,
    and shudder with sheer horror, says the
    LORD.
Two evils have my people done:
    they have forsaken me, the source of
    living waters;
They have dug themselves cisterns,
    broken cisterns, that hold no water.

The word of the Lord.

---

122. Jer 7:21-26

A reading from the Book of the Prophet Jeremiah

Listen to my voice; then I will be your God
and you shall be my people.

Thus says the LORD of hosts, the God of Is-
    rael:
    Heap your burnt offerings upon your
    sacrifices;
    eat up the flesh!
In speaking to your fathers
    on the day I brought them out of the land
    of Egypt,
    I gave them no command concerning
    burnt offering or sacrifice.
This rather is what I commanded them:
    Listen to my voice;
    then I will be your God
    and you shall be my people.

Walk in all the ways that I command you,
so that you may prosper.

But they obeyed not,
nor did they pay heed.

They walked in the hardness of their evil hearts
and turned their backs, not their faces, to me.

From the day that your fathers left the land of Egypt even to this day,
I have sent you untiringly all my servants the prophets.

Yet they have not obeyed me nor paid heed;
they have stiffened their necks and done worse than their fathers.

The word of the Lord.

---

123. Ez 11:14-21

A reading from the Book of the Prophet Ezekiel

I will remove the stony heart from their bodies,
and replace it with a natural heart,
so that they will live according to my statutes.

Thus the word of the LORD came to me:
Son of man, it is about your kinsmen,
your fellow exiles, and the whole house of Israel
that the inhabitants of Jerusalem say,
"They are far away from the LORD;
to us the land of Israel has been given as our possession."

Therefore say: Thus says the Lord GOD:
Though I have removed them far among the nations
and scattered them over foreign countries—
and was for a while their only sanctuary in the countries to which they had gone—
I will gather you from the nations
and assemble you from the countries over which you have been scattered,
and I will restore to you the land of Israel.

They shall return to it and remove from it all its detestable abominations.

I will give them a new heart and put a new spirit within them;
I will remove the stony heart from their bodies,

and replace it with a natural heart,
so that they will live according to my statutes,
and observe and carry out my ordinances;
thus they shall be my people and I will be their God.

But as for those whose hearts are devoted to their detestable abominations,
I will bring down their conduct upon their heads, says the Lord GOD.

The word of the Lord.

---

124. Ez 18:20-32

A reading from the Book of the Prophet Ezekiel

If the wicked man turns away from all the sins he committed,
he shall surely live, he shall not die.

The word of the Lord came to me thus:
Only the one who sins shall die.

The son shall not be charged with the guilt of his father,
nor shall the father be charged with the guilt of his son.

The virtuous man's virtue shall be his own,
as the wicked man's wickedness shall be his own.

But if the wicked man turns away from all the sins he committed,
if he keeps all my statutes and does what is right and just,
he shall surely live, he shall not die.

None of the crimes he committed shall be remembered against him;
he shall live because of the virtue he has practiced.

Do I indeed derive any pleasure from the death of the wicked?
says the Lord GOD.

Do I not rather rejoice
when he turns from his evil way that he may live?

And if the virtuous man turns from the path of virtue to do evil,
the same kind of abominable things that the wicked man does,
can he do this and still live?

None of his virtuous deeds shall be remembered,

because he has broken faith and committed sin;
because of this, he shall die.
You say, "The Lord's way is not fair!"
Hear now, house of Israel:
Is it my way that is unfair,
or rather, are not your ways unfair?
When a virtuous man turns away from
virtue to commit iniquity, and dies,
it is because of the iniquity he committed
that he must die.
But if a wicked man, turning from the
wickedness he has committed,
does what is right and just,
he shall preserve his life;
since he has turned away from all the sins
which he committed,
he shall surely live, he shall not die.
And yet the house of Israel says,
"The Lord's way is not fair!"
Is it my way that is not fair, house of Israel,
or rather, is it not that your ways are not
fair?
Therefore I will judge you, house of Israel,
each one according to his ways, says the
Lord God.
Turn and be converted from all your crimes,
that they may be no cause of guilt for you.
Cast away from you all the crimes you have
committed,
and make for yourselves a new heart and
a new spirit.
Why should you die, O house of Israel?
For I have no pleasure in the death of anyone who dies, says the Lord God.
Return and live!

The word of the Lord.

---

125. Ez 36:23-28

A reading from the Book of the
Prophet Ezekiel

*I will sprinkle clean water upon you and place a new spirit
within you and make you live by my statutes.*

Thus says the Lord:
I will prove the holiness of my great name,
profaned among the nations,
in whose midst you have profaned it.
Thus the nations shall know that I am the
Lord, says the Lord God,

when in their sight I prove my holiness
through you.
For I will take you away from among the nations,
gather you from all the foreign lands,
and bring you back to your own land.
I will sprinkle clean water upon you
to cleanse you from all your impurities,
and from all your idols I will cleanse you.
I will give you a new heart and place a new
spirit within you,
taking from your bodies your stony hearts
and giving you natural hearts.
I will put my spirit within you and make you
live by my statutes,
careful to observe my decrees.
You shall live in the land I gave your fathers;
you shall be my people, and I will be your
God.

The word of the Lord.

---

126. Hos 2:16-25

A reading from the Book of the
Prophet Hosea

I will make a covenant for them on that day.

Thus says the Lord:
I will allure her;
I will lead her into the desert
and speak to her heart.
From there I will give her the vineyards she
had,
and the valley of Achor as a door of hope.
She shall respond there as in the days of her
youth,
when she came up from the land of Egypt.

On that day, says the Lord,
She shall call me "My husband,"
and never again "My baal."
Then will I remove from her mouth the
names of the Baals,
so that they shall no longer be invoked.
I will make a covenant for them on that day,
with the beasts of the field,
With the birds of the air,
and with the things that crawl on the
ground.
Bow and sword and war
I will destroy from the land,
and I will let them take their rest in secu-
rity.

I will espouse you to me forever:
  I will espouse you in right and in justice,
  in love and in mercy;
I will espouse you in fidelity,
  and you shall know the LORD.
On that day I will respond, says the LORD;
  I will respond to the heavens,
  and they shall respond to the earth;
The earth shall respond to the grain, and
    wine, and oil,
  and these shall respond to Jezreel.
I will sow him for myself in the land,
  and I will have pity on Lo-ruhama.
I will say to Lo-ammi, "You are my people,"
  and he shall say, "My God!"

> The word of the Lord.

---

127. Hos 11:1-11

**A reading from the Book of the
Prophet Hosea**

I took them in my arms; I drew them with human cords.

Thus says the Lord;
When Israel was a child I loved him,
  out of Egypt I called my son.
The more I called them,
  the farther they went from me,
Sacrificing to the Baals
  and burning incense to idols.
Yet it was I who taught Ephraim to walk,
  who took them in my arms;
I drew them with human cords,
  with bands of love;
I fostered them like one
  who raises an infant to his cheeks;
Yet, though I stooped to feed my child,
  they did not know that I was their healer.

He shall return to the land of Egypt,
  and Assyria shall be his king;
The sword shall begin with his cities
  and end by consuming his solitudes.
Because they refused to repent,
  their own counsels shall devour them.
His people are in suspense about returning
    to him;
  and God, though in unison they cry out to
    him,
  shall not raise them up.

How could I give you up, O Ephraim,
  or deliver you up, O Israel?

How could I treat you as Admah,
  or make you like Zeboiim?
My heart is overwhelmed,
  my pity is stirred.
I will not give vent to my blazing anger,
  I will not destroy Ephraim again;
For I am God and not man,
  the Holy One present among you;
  I will not let the flames consume you.

They shall follow the LORD,
  who roars like a lion;
When he roars,
  his sons shall come frightened from the
    west,
Out of Egypt they shall come trembling, like
    sparrows,
  from the land of Assyria, like doves;
And I will resettle them in their homes, says
    the LORD.

> The word of the Lord.

---

128. Hos 14:2-10

**A reading from the Book of the
Prophet Hosea**

Return, O Israel, to the LORD, your God.

Thus says the LORD:
Return, O Israel, to the LORD, your God;
  you have collapsed through your guilt.
Take with you words,
  and return to the LORD;
Say to him, "Forgive all iniquity,
  and receive what is good, that we may
    render
  as offerings the bullocks from our stalls.
Assyria will not save us,
nor shall we have horses to mount;
We shall say no more, 'Our god,'
  to the work of our hands;
  for in you the orphan finds compassion."

I will heal their defection, says the LORD,
  I will love them freely;
  for my wrath is turned away from them.
I will be like the dew for Israel:
  he shall blossom like the lily;
He shall strike root like the Lebanon
    cedar,
  and put forth his shoots.

His splendor shall be like the olive tree
  and his fragrance like the Lebanon
    cedar.
Again they shall dwell in his shade
  and raise grain;
They shall blossom like the vine,
  and his fame shall be like the wine of
    Lebanon.
Ephraim! What more has he to do with
    idols?
  I have humbled him, but I will prosper
    him.
"I am like a verdant cypress tree"—
  Because of me you bear fruit!

Let him who is wise understand these
    things;
  let him who is prudent know them.
Straight are the paths of the LORD,
  in them the just walk,
  but sinners stumble in them.

The word of the Lord.

---

129. Jl 2:12-19

A reading from the Book of the Prophet Joel

Return to me with your whole heart.

Even now, says the LORD,
  return to me with your whole heart,
  with fasting, and weeping, and mourn-
    ing;
Rend your hearts, not your garments,
  and return to the LORD, your God.
For gracious and merciful is he,
  slow to anger, rich in kindness,
  and relenting in punishment.
Perhaps he will again relent
  and leave behind him a blessing,
Offerings and libations
  for the LORD, your God.

Blow the trumpet in Zion!
  proclaim a fast,
  call an assembly;
Gather the people,
  notify the congregation;
Assemble the elders,
  gather the children
  and the infants at the breast;

Let the bridegroom quit his room
  and the bride her chamber.
Between the porch and the altar
  let the priests, the ministers of the LORD,
    weep,
And say, "Spare, O LORD, your people,
  and make not your heritage a reproach,
  with the nations ruling over them!
Why should they say among the peoples,
  'Where is their God?' "

Then the LORD was stirred to concern for his
    land
  and took pity on his people.
The LORD answered and said to his people:
See, I will send you
  grain, and wine, and oil,
  and you shall be filled with them;
No more will I make you
  a reproach among the nations.

The word of the Lord.

---

130. Mic 6:1-15

A reading from the Book of the Prophet Micah

Do the right and love goodness,
and walk humbly with your God.

Hear, then, what the LORD says:
Arise, present your plea before the moun-
    tains,
  and let the hills hear your voice!
Hear, O mountains, the plea of the LORD,
  pay attention, O foundations of the earth!
For the LORD has a plea against his people,
  and he enters into trial with Israel.

O my people, what have I done to you,
  or how have I wearied you? Answer me!
For I brought you up from the land of Egypt,
  from the place of slavery I released you;
And I sent before you Moses,
  Aaron, and Miriam.
My people, remember what Moab's King
    Balak planned,
  and how Balaam, the son of Beor, an-
    swered him
  . . . from Shittim to Gilgal,
  that you may know the just deeds of the
    LORD.

With what shall I come before the Lord,
  and bow before God most high?
Shall I come before him with burnt offer-
    ings,
  with calves a year old?
Will the Lord be pleased with thousands of
    rams,
  with myriad streams of oil?
Shall I give my first-born for my crime,
  the fruit of my body for the sin of my soul?
You have been told, O man, what is good,
  and what the Lord requires of you:
Only to do the right and to love goodness,
  and to walk humbly with your God.

Hark! the Lord cries to the city.
  (It is wisdom to fear your name!)
  Hear, O tribe and city council,
You whose rich men are full of violence,
  whose inhabitants speak falsehood
  with deceitful tongues in their heads!
Am I to bear any longer criminal hoard-
    ing
  and the meager ephah that is accursed?
Shall I acquit criminal balances,
  bags of false weights?

Rather I will begin to strike you
  with devastation because of your sins.
You shall sow, yet not reap,
  tread out the olive, yet pour no oil,
  and the grapes, yet drink no wine.

> The word of the Lord.

---

131. Mic 7:2-7, 18-20

**A reading from the Book of the
Prophet Micah**

*The Lord will again have compassion on us and
cast into the depths of the sea all our sins.*

The faithful are gone from the earth,
  among men the upright are no more!
They all lie in wait to shed blood,
  each one ensnares the other.
Their hands succeed at evil;
  the prince makes demands,
The judge is had for a price,
  the great man speaks as he pleases,
The best of them is like a brier,
  the most upright like a thorn hedge.

The day announced by your watchmen!
  your punishment has come;
  now is the time of your confusion.
Put no trust in a friend,
  have no confidence in a companion;
Against her who lies in your bosom
  guard the portals of your mouth.
For the son dishonors his father,
  the daughter rises up against her mother,
The daughter-in-law against her mother-
    in-law,
  and a man's enemies are those of his
    household.

But as for me, I will look to the Lord,
  I will put my trust in God my savior;
  my God will hear me!

Who is there like you, the God who re-
    moves guilt
  and pardons sin for the remnant of his
    inheritance;
Who does not persist in anger forever,
  but delights rather in clemency,
And will again have compassion on us,
  treading underfoot our guilt?
You will cast into the depths of the sea
  all our sins;
You will show faithfulness to Jacob,
  and grace to Abraham,
As you have sworn to our fathers
  from days of old.

> The word of the Lord.

---

132. Zec 1:1-6

**A reading from the Book of the
Prophet Zechariah**

Return to me and I will return to you.

In the second year of Darius,
  in the eighth month,
  the word of the Lord came to the
    prophet Zechariah,
  son of Berechiah, son of Iddo:
The Lord was indeed angry with your fa-
    thers. . .
  and say to them:
    Thus says the Lord of hosts:
    Return to me, says the Lord of hosts,
    and I will return to you, says the Lord of
      hosts.

Be not like your fathers whom the former
    prophets warned:
  Thus says the Lord of hosts:
  Turn from your evil ways and from your
    wicked deeds.
But they would not listen or pay attention
    to me, says the Lord.
Your fathers, where are they?
And the prophets, can they live forever?

But my words and my decrees,
    which I entrusted to my servants the
        prophets,
did not these overtake your fathers?
Then they repented and admitted:
    "The Lord of hosts has treated us
    according to our ways and deeds,
    just as he had determined he would."

The word of the Lord.

RESPONSORIAL PSALMS

133. Ps 13:2-3, 4-5, 6

℟. (6a) My hope, O Lord, is in your mercy.

How long, O Lord? Will you utterly forget
    me?
  How long will you hide your face from
    me?
How long shall I harbor sorrow in my soul,
  Grief in my heart day after day?
How long will my enemy triumph over me?

℟. My hope, O Lord, is in your mercy.

Look, answer me, O Lord, my God!
Give light to my eyes that I may not sleep
    in death
  lest my enemy say, "I have overcome
    him";
  lest my foes rejoice at my downfall.

℟. My hope, O Lord, is in your mercy.

Though I trusted in your mercy,
Let my heart rejoice in your salvation;
  let me sing of the Lord, "He has been
    good to me."

℟. My hope, O Lord, is in your mercy.

---

134. Ps 25:4-5ab, 6 and
7bc, 8-9, 10 and 14, 15-16

℟. (16a) Turn to me, Lord, and have mercy.

Your ways, O Lord, make known to me;
  teach me your paths,
Guide me in your truth and teach me,
  for you are God my savior.

℟. Turn to me, Lord, and have mercy.

Remember that your compassion, O Lord,
  and your kindness are from of old.
In your kindness remember me,
  because of your goodness, O Lord.

℟. Turn to me, Lord, and have mercy.

Good and upright is the Lord;
  thus he shows sinners the way.
He guides the humble to justice,
  he teaches the humble his way.

℟. Turn to me, Lord, and have mercy.

All the paths of the Lord are kindness and
    constancy
  toward those who keep his covenant and
    his decrees.
The friendship of the Lord is with those
    who fear him,
  and his covenant, for their instruction.

℟. Turn to me, Lord, and have mercy.

My eyes are ever toward the Lord,
  for he will free my feet from the snare.
Look toward me, and have pity on me,
  for I am alone and afflicted.

℟. Turn to me, Lord, and have mercy.

135. Ps 31:2-3a, 3b-4, 6

℟. (6a) You have redeemed us, Lord, God of truth.

In you, O LORD, I take refuge;
  let me never be put to shame.
In your justice rescue me,
  incline your ear to me,
  make haste to deliver me!

℟. You have redeemed us, Lord, God of truth.

Be my rock of refuge,
  a stronghold to give me safety.
You are my rock and my fortress;
  for your name's sake you will lead and
  guide me.

℟. You have redeemed us, Lord, God of truth.

Into your hands I commend my spirit;
  you will redeem me, O LORD, O faithful
  God.

℟. You have redeemed us, Lord, God of truth.

---

136. Ps 32:1-2, 5, 6, 7, 11

℟. (5c) Lord, forgive the wrong I have done.

Blessed is he whose fault is taken away,
  whose sin is covered.
Blessed the man to whom the LORD imputes not guilt,
  in whose spirit there is no guile.

℟. Lord, forgive the wrong I have done.

Then I acknowledged my sin to you,
  my guilt I covered not.
I said, "I confess my faults to the LORD,"
  and you took away the guilt of my sin.

℟. Lord, forgive the wrong I have done.

For this shall every faithful man pray to
  you
  in time of stress.
Though deep waters overflow,
  they shall not reach him.

℟. Lord, forgive the wrong I have done.

You are my shelter; from distress you will
  preserve me;
  with glad cries of freedom you will ring
  me round.

℟. Lord, forgive the wrong I have done.

Be glad in the LORD and rejoice, you just;
  exult all you upright of heart.

℟. Lord, forgive the wrong I have done.

---

137. Ps 36:6-7ab, 8-9, 10-11

℟. (8) How precious is your mercy, Lord.

O LORD, your mercy reaches to heaven;
  your faithfulness, to the clouds.
Our justice is like the mountain of God:
  your judgments like the mighty deep.

℟. How precious is your mercy, Lord.

How precious is your mercy, O God!
  the children of men take shadow in the
  refuge of your wings.
They have their fill of the prime gifts of
  your house;
  from your delightful stream you give
  them to drink.

℟. How precious is your mercy, Lord.

For with you is the fountain of life,
  and in your light we see light.
Keep up your mercy toward your friends,
  your just defense of the upright of heart.

℟. How precious is your mercy, Lord.

---

138. Ps 50:7-8, 14-15,
16-17, 18-19, 20-21, 22-23

℟. (23b) To the upright I will show the saving power of God.

"Hear, my people, and I will speak;
  Israel, I will testify against you;
    God, your God, am I.
Not for your sacrifices do I rebuke you,
  for your burnt offerings are before me
  always."

℟. To the upright I will show the saving
  power of God.

"Offer to God praise as your sacrifice
  and fulfill your vows to the Most High;

Then call upon me in times of distress;
 I will rescue you, and you shall glorify me."

℞. To the upright I will show the saving power of God.

But to the wicked man God says:
 "Why do you recite my statutes,
and profess my covenant with your mouth,
Though you hate discipline
 and cast my words behind you?"

℞. To the upright I will show the saving power of God.

"When you see a thief, you keep pace with him,
 and with adulterers you throw in your lot.
To your mouth you give free rein for evil,
you harness your tongue to deceit."

℞. To the upright I will show the saving power of God.

"You sit speaking against your brother,
 against your mother's son you spread rumors.
When you do these things, shall I be deaf to it?
 Or do you think that I am like yourself?
I will correct you by drawing them up before your eyes."

℞. To the upright I will show the saving power of God.

"Consider this, you who forget God,
 lest I rend you and there be no one to rescue you.
He that offers praise as a sacrifice glorifies me;
 and to him that goes the right way I will show the salvation of God."

℞. To the upright I will show the saving power of God.

---

139. Ps 51:3-4, 5-6ab, 7-8, 9-11, 12-13, 14 and 17, 19

℞. (see 14a) Give me back the joy of your salvation.

Have mercy on me, O God, in your goodness;
 in the greatness of your compassion wipe out my offense.
Thoroughly wash me from my guilt
 and of my sin cleanse me.

℞. Give me back the joy of your salvation.

For I acknowledge my offense,
 and my sin is before me always:
"Against you only have I sinned,
 and done what is evil in your sight."

℞. Give me back the joy of your salvation.

Indeed, in guilt was I born,
 and in sin my mother conceived me;
Behold, you are pleased with sincerity of heart,
 and in my inmost being you teach me wisdom.

℞. Give me back the joy of your salvation.

Cleanse me of sin with hyssop, that I may be purified;
 Wash me, and I shall be whiter than snow.
Let me hear the sounds of joy and gladness;
 the bones you have crushed shall rejoice.
Turn away your face from my sins,
 and blot out all my guilt.

℞. Give me back the joy of your salvation.

A clean heart create for me, O God,
 and a steadfast spirit renew within me.
Cast me not out from your presence,
 and your Holy Spirit take not from me.

℞. Give me back the joy of your salvation.

Give me back the joy of your salvation,
 and a willing spirit sustain in me.

O Lord, open my lips,
  and my mouth shall proclaim your
  praise.

℟. Give me back the joy of your salvation.

My sacrifice, O God, is a contrite spirit;
  a heart contrite and humbled, O God,
  you will not spurn.

℟. Give me back the joy of your salvation.

---

140. Ps 73:1-2, 21-22a,
23-24, 26 and 28ab

℟. (28a) It is good for me to be with the
Lord.

How good God is to the upright;
  the LORD to those who are clean of heart!
But, as for me, I almost lost my balance;
  my feet all but slipped.

℟. It is good for me to be with the Lord.

Because my heart was embittered
  and my soul was pierced,
I was stupid and understood not.

℟. It is good for me to be with the Lord.

Yet with you I shall always be;
  you have hold of my right hand;
With your counsel you guide me,
  and in the end you will receive me in
  glory.

℟. It is good for me to be with the Lord.

Though my flesh and my heart waste
  away,
  God is the rock of my heart and my portion forever.
But for me, to be near God is my good;
  to make the Lord GOD my refuge.

℟. It is good for me to be with the Lord.

---

141. Ps 90:3-5a, 12-13,
14 and 17

℟. (14) Fill us with your love, O Lord, and
we will sing for joy!

You turn man back to dust,
  saying, "Return, O children of men."

For a thousand years in your sight
  are as yesterday, now that it is past,
  or as a watch of the night.

℟. Fill us with your love, O Lord, and we
will sing for joy!

Teach us to number our days aright,
  that we may gain wisdom of heart.
Return, O LORD! How long?
  Have pity on your servants!

℟. Fill us with your love, O Lord, and we
will sing for joy!

Fill us at daybreak with your kindness,
  that we may shout for joy and gladness
  all our days.
And may the gracious care of the LORD our
  God be ours;
  prosper the work of our hands for us!
  Prosper the work of our hands!

℟. Fill us with your love, O Lord, and we
will sing for joy!

---

142. Ps 95:1-2, 6-7c,
8-9, 10-11

℟. (8a) If today you hear his voice, harden
not your hearts.

Come, let us sing joyfully to the LORD;
  let us acclaim the Rock of our salvation.
Let us come into his presence with thanksgiving;
  let us joyfully sing psalms to him.

℟. If today you hear his voice, harden not
your hearts.

Come, let us bow down in worship;
  let us kneel before the LORD who made
  us.
For he is our God,
  and we are the people he shepherds, the
  flock he guides.

℟. If today you hear his voice, harden not
your hearts.

Oh, that today you would hear his voice:
  "Harden not your hearts as at Meribah,
  as in the day of Massah in the desert,

Where your fathers tempted me;
  they tested me though they had seen my
  works.”

℟. If today you hear his voice, harden not
  your hearts.

Forty years I was wearied of that genera-
tion;
  I said: “This people’s heart goes astray,
  they do not know my ways.”
Therefore I swore in my anger:
  “They shall never enter my rest.”

℟. If today you hear his voice, harden not
  your hearts.

---

143. Ps 119:1, 10-11, 12-13, 15-16

℟. (1) Blessed are they who follow the law of
  the Lord!

Blessed are they whose way is blameless,
  who walk in the way of the Lord.

℟. Blessed are they who follow the law of
  the Lord!

With all my heart I seek you;
  let me not stray from your commands.
Within my heart I treasure your promise.
  that I may not sin against you.

℟. Blessed are they who follow the law of
  the Lord!

Blessed are you, O Lord;
  teach me your statutes.
With my lips I declare
  all the ordinances of your mouth.

℟. Blessed are they who follow the law of
  the Lord!

I will meditate on your precepts
  and consider your ways,
In your statutes I will delight;
  I will not forget your words.

℟. Blessed are they who follow the law of
  the Lord!

---

144. Ps 123:1-2a, 2bc, 3-4

℟. (2c) Our eyes are fixed on the Lord.

To you I lift up my eyes
  who are enthroned in heaven —
As the eyes of servants
  are on the hands of their masters.

℟. Our eyes are fixed on the Lord.

As the eyes of a maid
  are on the hands of her mistress,
So are our eyes on the Lord, our God,
  till he have pity on us.

℟. Our eyes are fixed on the Lord.

Have pity on us, O Lord, have pity on us,
  for we are more than sated with contempt;
Our souls are more than sated
  with the mockery of the arrogant,
  with the contempt of the proud.

℟. Our eyes are fixed on the Lord.

---

145. Ps 130:1-2, 3-4, 5-6, 7-8

℟. (7bc) With the Lord there is mercy and
  fullness of redemption.

Out of the depths I cry to you, O Lord;
  Lord, hear my voice!
Let your ears be attentive
  to my voice in supplication.

℟. With the Lord there is mercy and fullness of redemption.

If you, O Lord, mark iniquities,
  Lord, who can stand?
But with you is forgiveness,
  that you may be revered.

℟. With the Lord there is mercy and fullness of redemption.

I trust in the Lord;
  my soul trusts in his word.
More than sentinels wait for the dawn,
  let Israel wait for the Lord.

℟. With the Lord there is mercy and fullness of redemption.

For with the Lord is kindness
  and with him is plenteous redemption;

And he will redeem Israel
  from all their iniquities.

℟. With the Lord there is mercy and fullness of redemption.

------

146. Ps 139:1-3, 4-6, 7-8, 9-10,
11-12, 13-14ab, 14c-15, 16,
17-18, 23-24

℟. (23a) You have searched me, and you know me, Lord.

O LORD, you have probed me and you know me;
  you know when I sit and when I stand;
  you understand my thoughts from afar.
My journeys and my rest you scrutinize,
  with all my ways you are familiar.

℟. You have searched me, and you know me, Lord.

Even before a word is on my tongue,
  behold, O LORD, you know the whole of it.
Behind me and before, you hem me in
  and rest your hand upon me.
Such knowledge is too wonderful for me;
  too lofty for me to attain.

℟. You have searched me, and you know me, Lord.

Where can I go from your spirit?
  from your presence where can I flee?
If I go up to the heavens, you are there;
  if I sink to the nether world, you are present there.

℟. You have searched me, and you know me, Lord.

If I take the wings of the dawn;
  if I settle at the farthest limits of the sea
Even there your hand shall guide me,
  and your right hand hold me fast.

℟. You have searched me, and you know me, Lord.

If I say, "Surely the darkness shall hide me,
  and night shall be my light"—
For you darkness itself is not dark,
  and night shines as the day.
  darkness and light are the same.

℟. You have searched me, and you know me, Lord.

Truly you have formed my inmost being;
  you knit me in my mother's womb.
I give you thanks that I am fearfully, wonderfully made;
  wonderful are your works.

℟. You have searched me, and you know me, Lord.

My soul also you knew full well;
  nor was my frame unknown to you
When I was made in secret,
  when I was fashioned in the depths of the earth.

℟. You have searched me, and you know me, Lord.

Your eyes have seen my actions;
  in your book they are all written;
  my days were limited before one of them existed.

℟. You have searched me, and you know me, Lord.

How weighty are your designs, O God,
  how vast the sum of them.
Were I to recount them, they would outnumber the sands;
  did I reach the end of them, I should still be with you.

℟. You have searched me, and you know me, Lord.

Probe me, O God, and know my heart,
  try me, and know my thoughts;
See if my way is crooked,
  and lead me in the way of old.

℟. You have searched me, and you know me, Lord.

------

147. Ps 143:1-2, 5-6, 7ab
and 8ab, 10

℟. (10a) Teach me to do your will, my God.

O Lord, hear my prayer;
  hearken to my pleading in your faithfulness;
  in your justice answer me.
And enter not into judgment with your servant,
  for before you no living man is just.

℟. Teach me to do your will, my God.

For the enemy pursues me;
  he has crushed my life to the ground;
He has left me dwelling in the dark like
  those long dead.
  and my spirit is faint within me,
  my heart within me is appalled.

℟. Teach me to do your will, my God.

I remember the days of old;
  I meditate on all your doings;
  the works of your hands I ponder.
I stretch out my hands to you;
  my soul thirsts for you like parched land.

℟. Teach me to do your will, my God.

Hasten to answer me, O Lord;
  for my spirit fails me.
Hide not your face from me
  lest I become like those who go down
  into the pit.
At dawn let me hear of your mercy,
  for in you I trust.

℟. Teach me to do your will, my God.

Show me the way in which I should walk,
  for to you I lift up my soul.
Rescue me from my enemies, O Lord,
  for in you I hope.

℟. Teach me to do your will, my God.

Teach me to do your will,
  for you are my God.
May your good spirit guide me
  on level ground.

℟. Teach me to do your will, my God.

For your name's sake, O Lord, preserve
  me;
  in your justice free me from distress.

℟. Teach me to do your will, my God.

_____

READINGS FROM THE NEW TESTAMENT

148. Rom 3:22-26

**A reading from the Letter of
Saint Paul to the Romans**

They are justified freely by his grace through
the redemption in Christ Jesus.

Brothers and sisters:
The righteousness of God through faith in
  Jesus Christ is
  for all who believe.
For there is no distinction;
  all have sinned and are deprived of the
  glory of God.
They are justified freely by his grace
  through the redemption in Christ Jesus,
  whom God set forth as an expiation,
  through faith, by his Blood, to prove his
  righteousness
  because of the forgiveness of sins previ-
  ously committed,

through the forbearance of God—
  to prove his righteousness in the present
  time,
  that he might be righteous
  and justify the one who has faith in
  Jesus.

The word of the Lord.

_____

149. Rom 5:6-11

**A reading from the Letter of
Saint Paul to the Romans**

We boast of God through our Lord Jesus Christ,
through whom we have now received reconciliation.

Brothers and sisters:
Christ, while we were still helpless,
  yet died at the appointed time for the un-
  godly.
Indeed, only with difficulty does one die
  for a just person,

though perhaps for a good person
one might even find courage to die.
But God proves his love for us
in that while we were still sinners Christ
died for us.
How much more then, since we are now
justified by his Blood,
will we be saved through him from the
wrath.
Indeed, if, while we were enemies,
we were reconciled to God through the
death of his Son,
how much more, once reconciled,
will we be saved by his life.
Not only that,
but we also boast of God through our
Lord Jesus Christ,
through whom we have now received
reconciliation.

The word of the Lord.

---

150. Rom 6:2-11

A reading from the Letter of Saint Paul to the Romans

You must think of yourselves as being dead to sin and living for God in Christ Jesus.

Brothers and sisters:
How can we who died to sin yet live in it?
Are you unaware that we who were baptized into Christ Jesus
were baptized into his death?
We were indeed buried with him through
baptism into death,
so that, just as Christ was raised from
the dead
by the glory of the Father,
we too might live in newness of life.

For if we have grown into union with him
through a death like his,
we shall also be united with him in the
resurrection.
We know that our old self was crucified
with him,
so that our sinful body might be done
away with,
that we might no longer be in slavery to
sin.
For a dead person has been absolved from
sin.

If, then, we have died with Christ,
we believe that we shall also live with
him.
We know that Christ, raised from the dead,
dies no more;
death no longer has power over him.
As to his death, he died to sin once and for
all;
as to his life, he lives for God.
Consequently, you too must think of yourselves as being dead to sin
and living for God in Christ Jesus.

The word of the Lord.

---

151. Rom 6:12-23

A reading from the Letter of Saint Paul to the Romans

For the wages of sin is death, but the gift of God is eternal life in Christ Jesus our Lord.

Brothers and sisters:
Sin must not reign over your mortal bodies
so that you obey their desires.
And do not present the parts of your bodies to sin
as weapons for wickedness,
but present yourselves to God as raised
from the dead to life
and the parts of your bodies to God
as weapons for righteousness.
For sin is not to have any power over you,
since you are not under the law but
under grace.

What then? Shall we sin because we are
not under the law
but under grace?
Of course not!
Do you not know that if you present yourselves
to someone as obedient slaves,
you are slaves of the one you obey,
either of sin, which leads to death,
or of obedience, which leads to righteousness?
But thanks be to God that, although you
were once slaves of sin,
you have become obedient from the
heart
to the pattern of teaching to which you
were entrusted.

Freed from sin, you have become slaves of
righteousness.
I am speaking in human terms because of
the weakness of your nature.
For just as you presented the parts of your
bodies as slaves to impurity
and to lawlessness for lawlessness,
so now present them as slaves to righteousness for sanctification.
For when you were slaves of sin, you were
free from righteousness.
But what profit did you get then
from the things of which you are now
ashamed?
For the end of those things is death.
But now that you have been freed from sin
and have become slaves of God,
the benefit that you have leads to sanctification,
and its end is eternal life.
For the wages of sin is death,
but the gift of God is eternal life in Christ
Jesus our Lord.

The word of the Lord.

---

152. Rom 7:14-25a

A reading from the Letter of
Saint Paul to the Romans

Miserable one that I am! Who will deliver me from this mortal
body? Thanks be to God through Jesus Christ our Lord.

Brothers and sisters:
We know that the law is spiritual;
but I am carnal, sold into slavery to sin.
What I do, I do not understand.
For I do not do what I want,
but I do what I hate.
Now if I do what I do not want,
I concur that the law is good.
So now it is no longer I who do it,
but sin that dwells in me.
I know that good does not dwell in me,
that is, in my flesh.
The willing is ready at hand, but doing the
good is not.
For I do not do the good I want,
but I do the evil I do not want.
Now if I do what I do not want, it is no
longer I who do it,
but sin that dwells in me.

So, then, I discover the principle
that when I want to do right, evil is at
hand.
For I take delight in the law of God, in my
inner self,
but I see in my members another principle
at war with the law of my mind,
taking me captive to the law of sin that
dwells in my members.
Miserable one that I am!
Who will deliver me from this mortal
body?
Thanks be to God through Jesus Christ our
Lord.

The word of the Lord.

---

153. Rom 12:1-2, 9-18

A reading from the Letter of
Saint Paul to the Romans

Be transformed by the renewal of your mind.

I urge you, brothers and sisters, by the mercies of God,
to offer your bodies as a living sacrifice,
holy and pleasing to God, your spiritual
worship.
Do not conform yourselves to this age
but be transformed by the renewal of your
mind,
that you may discern what is the will of
God,
what is good and pleasing and perfect.
Let love be sincere;
hate what is evil,
hold on to what is good;
love one another with mutual affection;
anticipate one another in showing honor.
Do not grow slack in zeal,
be fervent in spirit,
serve the Lord.
Rejoice in hope,
endure in affliction,
persevere in prayer.
Contribute to the needs of the holy ones,
exercise hospitality.
Bless those who persecute you,
bless and do not curse them.

Rejoice with those who rejoice,
  weep with those who weep.
Have the same regard for one another;
  do not be haughty but associate with the
    lowly;
  do not be wise in your own estimation.
Do not repay anyone evil for evil;
  be concerned for what is noble in the sight
    of all.
If possible, on your part, live at peace with
  all.
Beloved, do not look for revenge
  but leave room for the wrath;
  for it is written,
  *Vengeance is mine, I will repay, says the
    Lord.*

> The word of the Lord.

154. Rom 13:8-14

A reading from the Letter of
Saint Paul to the Romans

Throw off the works of darkness
and put on the armor of light.

Brothers and sisters:
Owe nothing to anyone, except to love one
  another;
  for the one who loves another has ful-
    filled the law.
The commandments, *You shall not commit
    adultery;*
  you shall not kill; you shall not steal;
  you shall not covet,
  and whatever other commandment there
    may be,
  are summed up in this saying, namely,
  *You shall love your neighbor as your-
    self.*
Love does no evil to the neighbor;
  hence, love is the fulfillment of the law.
And do this because you know the time;
  it is the hour now for you to awake from
    sleep.
For our salvation is nearer now than when
    we first believed;
  the night is advanced, the day is at hand.
Let us then throw off the works of darkness
  and put on the armor of light;

let us conduct ourselves properly as in
    the day,
  not in orgies and drunkenness,
  not in promiscuity and lust,
  not in rivalry and jealousy.
But put on the Lord Jesus Christ,
  and make no provision for the desires of
    the flesh.

> The word of the Lord.

155. 2 Cor 5:17-21

A reading from the second Letter of
Saint Paul to the Corinthians

God was reconciling the world to himself in Christ.

Brothers and sisters:
Whoever is in Christ is a new creation:
  the old things have passed away;
  behold, new things have come.
And all this is from God,
  who has reconciled us to himself through
    Christ
  and given us the ministry of reconcilia-
    tion,
  namely, God was reconciling the world to
    himself in Christ,
  not counting their trespasses against them
  and entrusting to us the message of recon-
    ciliation.
So we are ambassadors for Christ,
  as if God were appealing through us.
We implore you on behalf of Christ,
  be reconciled to God.
For our sake he made him to be sin who did
    not know sin,
  so that we might become the righteous-
    ness of God in him.

> The word of the Lord.

156. Gal 5:16-24

A reading from the Letter of Saint Paul to the Galatians

Those who belong to Christ Jesus have crucified their flesh with its passions and desires.

Brothers and sisters, live by the Spirit
  and you will certainly not gratify the desire of the flesh.
For the flesh has desires against the Spirit,
  and the Spirit against the flesh;
  these are opposed to each other,
  so that you may not do what you want.
But if you are guided by the Spirit, you are
  not under the law.
Now the works of the flesh are obvious:
  immorality, impurity, lust, idolatry,
  sorcery, hatreds, rivalry, jealousy,
  outbursts of fury, acts of selfishness,
  dissensions, factions, occasions of envy,
  drinking bouts, orgies, and the like.
I warn you, as I warned you before,
  that those who do such things will not
  inherit the Kingdom of God.
In contrast, the fruit of the Spirit is love,
  joy, peace,
  patience, kindness, generosity,
  faithfulness, gentleness, self-control.
Against such there is no law.
Now those who belong to Christ Jesus
  have crucified their flesh
  with its passions and desires.

The word of the Lord.

---

157. Eph 2:1-10

A reading from the Letter of Saint Paul to the Ephesians

God, because of the great love he had for us, even when we were dead in our transgressions, brought us to life with Christ.

Brothers and sisters:
You were dead in your transgressions and
  sins
  in which you once lived following the age
  of this world,
  following the ruler of the power of the air,
  the spirit that is now at work in the disobedient.

All of us once lived among them in the desires of our flesh,
  following the wishes of the flesh and the
  impulses,
  and we were by nature children of wrath,
  like the rest.
But God, who is rich in mercy,
  because of the great love he had for us,
  even when we were dead in our transgressions,
  brought us to life with Christ (by grace
  you have been saved),
  raised us up with him,
  and seated us with him in the heavens in
  Christ Jesus,
  that in the ages to come
he might show the immeasurable riches of
  his grace
  in his kindness to us in Christ Jesus.
For by grace you have been saved through
  faith,
  and this is not from you; it is the gift of
  God;
  it is not from works, so no one may boast.
For we are his handiwork, created in Christ
  Jesus for good works
  that God has prepared in advance,
  that we should live in them.

The word of the Lord.

---

158. Eph 4:1-3, 17-32

A reading from the Letter of Saint Paul to the Ephesians

Be renewed in the spirit of your minds, and put on the new self.

I, then, a prisoner for the Lord,
  urge you to live in a manner
  worthy of the call you have received,
  with all humility and gentleness,
  with patience,
  bearing with one another through love,
  striving to preserve the unity of the spirit
  through the bond of peace:
So I declare and testify in the Lord
  that you must no longer live as the Gentiles do,
  in the futility of their minds;
  darkened in understanding,

alienated from the life of God because of
their ignorance,
because of their hardness of heart,
they have become callous
and have handed themselves over to licentiousness
for the practice of every kind of impurity
to excess.
That is not how you learned Christ,
assuming that you have heard of him
and were taught in him,
as truth is in Jesus,
that you should put away the old self of
your former way of life,
corrupted through deceitful desires,
and be renewed in the spirit of your
minds,
and put on the new self,
created in God's way in righteousness and
holiness of truth.

Therefore, putting away falsehood,
speak the truth,
each one to his neighbor,
for we are members one of another.
Be angry but do not sin;
do not let the sun set on your anger,
and do not leave room for the Devil.
The thief must no longer steal,
but rather labor,
doing honest work with his own hands,
so that he may have something to share
with one in need.
No foul language should come out of your
mouths,
but only such as is good for needed edification,
that it may impart grace to those who
hear.
And do not grieve the Holy Spirit of God,
with which you were sealed for the day of
redemption.
All bitterness, fury, anger, shouting, and reviling
must be removed from you,
along with all malice.
And be kind to one another, compassionate,
forgiving one another as God has forgiven
you in Christ.

The word of the Lord.

---

159. Eph 5:1-14

A reading from the Letter of Saint Paul to the Ephesians

*You were once darkness, but now you are light in the Lord.
Live as children of light.*

Brothers and sisters:
Be imitators of God, as beloved children,
and live in love,
as Christ loved us and handed himself
over for us
as a sacrificial offering to God for a fragrant aroma.
Immorality or any impurity or greed
must not even be mentioned among you,
as is fitting among holy ones,
no obscenity or silly or suggestive talk,
which is out of place,
but instead, thanksgiving.
Be sure of this,
that no immoral or impure or greedy
person, that is, an idolater,
has any inheritance in the Kingdom of
Christ and of God.

Let no one deceive you with empty arguments,
for because of these things
the wrath of God is coming upon the disobedient.
So do not be associated with them.
For you were once darkness,
but now you are light in the Lord.
Live as children of light,
for light produces every kind of goodness and righteousness and truth.
Try to learn what is pleasing to the Lord.
Take no part in the fruitless works of darkness;
rather expose them,
for it is shameful even to mention the
things done by them in secret;
but everything exposed by the light becomes visible,
for everything that becomes visible is
light.
Therefore, it says:
"Awake, O sleeper,
and arise from the dead,
and Christ will give you light."

The word of the Lord.

160. Eph 6:10-18

A reading from the Letter of Saint Paul to the Ephesians

Put on the armor of God,
that you may be able to resist on the evil day.

Brothers and sisters:
Draw your strength from the Lord and
from his mighty power.
Put on the armor of God so that you may
be able to stand firm
against the tactics of the Devil.
For our struggle is not with flesh and blood
but with the principalities, with the powers,
with the world rulers of this present darkness,
with the evil spirits in the heavens.
Therefore, put on the armor of God,
that you may be able to resist on the evil
day
and, having done everything, to hold your
ground.
So stand fast with your loins girded in truth,
clothed with righteousness as a breast-
plate,
and your feet shod in readiness for the
Gospel of peace.
In all circumstances, hold faith as a shield,
to quench all the flaming arrows of the
Evil One.
And take the helmet of salvation and the
sword of the Spirit,
which is the word of God.

With all prayer and supplication,
pray at every opportunity in the Spirit.
To that end, be watchful with all perseverance and supplication
for all the holy ones.

The word of the Lord.

---

161. Col 3:1-10, 12-17

A reading from the Letter of Saint Paul to the Colossians

If you were raised with Christ, seek what is above.
Put to death, then, the parts of you that are earthly.

Brothers and sisters:
If you were raised with Christ, seek what
is above,

where Christ is seated at the right hand
of God.
Think of what is above, not of what is on
earth.
For you have died, and your life is hidden
with Christ in God.
When Christ your life appears,
then you too will appear with him in
glory.
Put to death, then, the parts of you that are
earthly:
immorality, impurity, passion, evil desire,
and the greed that is idolatry.
Because of these the wrath of God is coming upon the disobedient.
By these you too once conducted yourselves, when you lived in that way.
But now you must put them all away:
anger, fury, malice, slander,
and obscene language out of your
mouths.
Stop lying to one another,
since you have taken off the old self with
its practices
and have put on the new self,
which is being renewed, for knowledge,
in the image of its creator.

Put on, as God's chosen ones, holy and
beloved,
heartfelt compassion, kindness, humility,
gentleness, and patience,
bearing with one another and forgiving
one another,
if one has a grievance against another;
as the Lord has forgiven you, so must
you also do.
And over all these put on love,
that is, the bond of perfection.
And let the peace of Christ control your
hearts,
the peace into which you were also
called in one Body.
And be thankful.
Let the word of Christ dwell in you richly,
as in all wisdom you teach and admonish
one another,
singing psalms, hymns, and spiritual
songs
with gratitude in your hearts to God.

And whatever you do, in word or in deed,
do everything in the name of the Lord Jesus,
giving thanks to God the Father through him.

The word of the Lord.

---

162. Heb 12:1-5

**A reading from the Letter
to the Hebrews**

*In your struggle against sin you have not yet resisted
to the point of shedding blood.*

Brothers and sisters:
Since we are surrounded by so great a cloud of witnesses,
let us rid ourselves of every burden and sin that clings to us
and persevere in running the race that lies before us
while keeping our eyes fixed on Jesus, the leader and perfecter of faith.
For the sake of the joy that lay before him
Jesus endured the cross, despising its shame,
and has taken his seat at the right of the throne of God.
Consider how he endured such opposition from sinners,
in order that you may not grow weary and lose heart.
In your struggle against sin
you have not yet resisted to the point of shedding blood.
You have also forgotten the exhortation addressed to you as sons:
My son, do not disdain the discipline of the Lord
or lose heart when reproved by him.

The word of the Lord.

---

163. Jas 1:22-27

A reading from the Letter of Saint James

Be doers of the word and not hearers only.

Beloved:
Be doers of the word and not hearers only, deluding yourselves.
For if anyone is a hearer of the word and not a doer,
he is like a man who looks at his own face in a mirror.
He sees himself, then goes off and promptly forgets
what he looked like.
But the one who peers into the perfect law of freedom and perseveres,
and is not a hearer who forgets but a doer who acts;
such a one shall be blessed in what he does.
If anyone thinks he is religious and does not bridle his tongue
but deceives his heart, his religion is vain.
Religion that is pure and undefiled before God and the Father is this:
to care for orphans and widows in their affliction
and to keep oneself unstained by the world.

The word of the Lord.

---

164. Jas 2:14-26

A reading from the Letter of Saint James

*What good is it if someone says he has faith
but does not have works?*

What good is it, my brothers and sisters,
if someone says he has faith but does not have works?
Can that faith save him?
If a brother or sister has nothing to wear
and has no food for the day,
and one of you says to them,
"Go in peace, keep warm, and eat well,"
but you do not give them the necessities of the body,
what good is it?
So also faith of itself,
if it does not have works, is dead.
Indeed someone might say,
"You have faith and I have works."
Demonstrate your faith to me without works,
and I will demonstrate my faith to you from my works.
You believe that God is one.
You do well.

Even the demons believe that and tremble.
Do you want proof, you ignoramus,
    that faith without works is useless?
Was not Abraham our father justified by
        works
    when he offered his son Isaac upon the
        altar?
You see that faith was active along with
        his works,
    and faith was completed by the works.
Thus the Scripture was fulfilled that says,
    Abraham believed God,
    and it was credited to him as righteous-
        ness,
    and he was called *the friend of God.*
See how a person is justified by works and
        not by faith alone.
And in the same way, was not Rahab the
        harlot also justified by works
    when she welcomed the messengers
    and sent them out by a different route?
For just as a body without a spirit is dead,
    so also faith without works is dead.

The word of the Lord.

---

165. Jas 3:1-12

A reading from the Letter of Saint James

If anyone does not fall short in speech,
he is a perfect man.

Not many of you should become teachers,
        my brothers and sisters,
    for you realize that we will be judged
        more strictly,
    for we all fall short in many respects.
If anyone does not fall short in speech, he
        is a perfect man,
    able to bridle the whole body also.
If we put bits into the mouths of horses to
        make them obey us,
    we also guide their whole bodies.
It is the same with ships:
    even though they are so large and driven
        by fierce winds,
    they are steered by a very small rud-
        der
    wherever the pilot's inclination wishes.
In the same way the tongue is a small
        member
    and yet has great pretensions.

Consider how small a fire can set a huge for-
        est ablaze.
The tongue is also a fire.
It exists among our members as a world of
        malice,
    defiling the whole body
    and setting the entire course of our lives
        on fire,
    itself set on fire by Gehenna.
For every kind of beast and bird, of reptile
        and sea creature,
    can be tamed and has been tamed by the
        human species,
    but no man can tame the tongue.
It is a restless evil, full of deadly poison.
With it we bless the Lord and Father,
    and with it we curse men
    who are made in the likeness of God.
From the same mouth come blessing and
        cursing.
My brothers and sisters, this need not be so.
Does a spring gush forth from the same
        opening
    both pure and brackish water?
Can a fig tree, my brothers and sisters, pro-
        duce olives,
    or a grapevine figs?
Neither can salt water yield fresh.

The word of the Lord.

---

166. 1 Pt 1:13-23

A reading from the first Letter
of Saint Peter

You were ransomed not with perishable things
like silver or gold but with the precious Blood of Christ
as of a spotless unblemished Lamb.

Beloved:
Gird up the loins of your mind, live soberly,
    and set your hopes completely on the
        grace to be brought to you
    at the revelation of Jesus Christ.
Like obedient children,
    do not act in compliance with the desires
        of your former ignorance
    but, as he who called you is holy,
    be holy yourselves in every aspect of your
        conduct,
    for it is written, *Be holy because I am*
    holy.

Realize that you were ransomed from your
futile conduct,
handed on by your ancestors,
not with perishable things like silver or
gold
but with the precious Blood of Christ
as of a spotless unblemished Lamb.
He was known before the foundation of the
world
but revealed in the final time for you,
who through him believe in God
who raised him from the dead and gave
him glory,
so that your faith and hope are in God.

Since you have purified yourselves
by obedience to the truth for sincere
brotherly love,
love one another intensely from a pure
heart.
You have been born anew,
not from perishable but from imperish-
able seed,
through the living and abiding word of
God.

The word of the Lord.

---

167. 2 Pt 1:3-11

A reading from the second Letter
of Saint Peter

Be all the more eager to make your call and election firm.

Beloved:
His divine power has bestowed on us
everything that makes for life and devotion,
through the knowledge of him
who called us by his own glory and power.
Through these, he has bestowed on us
the precious and very great promises,
so that through them you may come to
share in the divine nature,
after escaping from the corruption that
is in the world
because of evil desire.
For this very reason,
make every effort to supplement your
faith with virtue,
virtue with knowledge, knowledge with
self-control,

self-control with endurance, endurance
with devotion,
devotion with mutual affection, mutual
affection with love.
If these are yours and increase in abundance,
they will keep you from being idle or un-
fruitful
in the knowledge of our Lord Jesus
Christ.
Anyone who lacks them is blind and short-
sighted,
forgetful of the cleansing of his past sins.
Therefore, brothers and sisters, be all the
more eager
to make your call and election firm,
for, in doing so, you will never stumble.
For, in this way, entry into the eternal
Kingdom
of our Lord and savior Jesus Christ
will be richly provided for you.

The word of the Lord.

---

168. 1 Jn 1:5—2:2

A reading from the first Letter
of Saint John

If we acknowledge our sins, he is faithful and just and
will forgive our sins and cleanse us from every wrongdoing.

Beloved:
This is the message that we have heard
from Jesus Christ
and proclaim to you: God is light,
and in him there is no darkness at all.
If we say, "We have fellowship with God,"
while we continue to walk in darkness,
we lie and do not act in truth.
But if we walk in the light as he is in the
light,
then we have fellowship with one another,
and the Blood of his Son Jesus cleanses
us from all sin.
If we say, "We are without sin," we deceive ourselves,
and the truth is not in us.
If we acknowledge our sins, he is faithful
and just
and will forgive our sins and cleanse us
from every wrongdoing.

If we say, "We have not sinned," we make him a liar,
  and his word is not in us.

My children, I am writing this to you so that you may not commit sin.
But if anyone does sin, we have an Advocate with the Father,
  Jesus Christ the righteous one.
He is expiation for our sins,
  and not for our sins only but for those of the whole world.

  The word of the Lord.

---

169. 1 Jn 2:3-11

A reading from the first Letter of Saint John

Whoever hates his brother, is still in the darkness.

Beloved:
The way we may be sure that we know Jesus
  is to keep his commandments.
Whoever says, "I know him," but does not keep his commandments
  is a liar, and the truth is not in him.
But whoever keeps his word,
  the love of God is truly perfected in him.
This is the way we may know that we are in union with him:
  whoever claims to abide in him ought to walk just as he walked.

Beloved, I am writing no new commandment to you
  but an old commandment that you had from the beginning.
The old commandment is the word that you have heard.
And yet I do write a new commandment to you,
  which holds true in him and among you,
  for the darkness is passing away,
  and the true light is already shining.
Whoever says he is in the light,
  yet hates his brother, is still in the darkness.
Whoever loves his brother remains in the light,
  and there is nothing in him to cause a fall.
Whoever hates his brother is in darkness;
  he walks in darkness

and does not know where he is going
  because the darkness has blinded his eyes.

  The word of the Lord.

---

170. 1 Jn 3:1-24

A reading from the first Letter of Saint John

We know that we have passed from death to life because we love our brothers.

See what love the Father has bestowed on us that we may be called the children of God.
Yet so we are.
The reason the world does not know us
  is that it did not know him.
Beloved, we are God's children now;
  what we shall be has not yet been revealed.
We do know that when it is revealed
  we shall be like him,
  for we shall see him as he is.
Everyone who has this hope based on him makes himself pure,
  as he is pure.
Everyone who commits sin commits lawlessness,
  for sin is lawlessness.
You know that he was revealed to take away sins,
  and in him there is no sin.
No one who remains in him sins;
  no one who sins has seen him or known him.
Children, let no one deceive you.
The person who acts in righteousness is righteous,
  just as he is righteous.
Whoever sins belongs to the Devil,
  because the Devil has sinned from the beginning.
Indeed, the Son of God was revealed to destroy the works of the Devil.
No one who is begotten by God commits sin,
  because God's seed remains in him;
  he cannot sin because he is begotten by God.
In this way, the children of God and the children of the Devil are made plain;

no one who fails to act in righteousness
belongs to God,
nor anyone who does not love his
brother.

For this is the message you have heard
from the beginning:
we should love one another,
unlike Cain who belonged to the Evil
One and slaughtered his brother.
Why did he slaughter him?
Because his own works were evil,
and those of his brother righteous.
Do not be amazed, then, brothers and sisters,
if the world hates you.
We know that we have passed from death
to life
because we love our brothers.
Whoever does not love remains in death.
Everyone who hates his brother is a murderer,
and you know that no murderer has
eternal life remaining in him.
The way we came to know love
was that he laid down his life for us;
so we ought to lay down our lives for our
brothers.
If someone who has worldly means sees a
brother in need
and refuses him compassion, how can
the love of God remain in him?
Children, let us love not in word or speech
but in deed and truth.
Now this is how we shall know that we belong to the truth
and reassure our hearts before him in
whatever our hearts condemn,
for God is greater than our hearts and
knows everything.
Beloved, if our hearts do not condemn us,
we have confidence in God
and receive from him whatever we ask,
because we keep his commandments
and do what pleases him.
And his commandment is this:
we should believe in the name of his
Son, Jesus Christ,
and love one another just as he commanded us.
Those who keep his commandments remain in him, and he in them,

and the way we know that he remains in
us
is from the Spirit that he gave us.

The word of the Lord.

---

171. 1 Jn 4:16-21

A reading from the first Letter of Saint John

God is love, and whoever remains in love remains in God
and God in him.

Beloved:
We have come to know and to believe in the
love God has for us.

God is love, and whoever remains in love remains in God and God in him.
In this is love brought to perfection among
us,
that we have confidence on the day of
judgment
because as he is, so are we in this world.
There is no fear in love,
but perfect love drives out fear
because fear has to do with punishment,
and so one who fears is not yet perfect in
love.
Beloved, we love God because
he first loved us.
If anyone says, "I love God,"
but hates his brother, he is a liar;
for whoever does not love a brother
whom he has seen
cannot love God whom he has not seen.
This is the commandment we have from
him:
Whoever loves God must also love his
brother.

The word of the Lord.

---

172. Rv 2:1-5

A reading from the Book of Revelation

Repent, and do the works you did at first.

To the angel of the Church in Ephesus,
write this:
" 'The one who holds the seven stars in
his right hand
and walks in the midst of the seven gold
lampstands says this:

"I know your works, your labor, and
     your endurance,
and that you cannot tolerate the wicked;
you have tested those who call them-
     selves apostles but are not,
and discovered that they are impostors.
Moreover, you have endurance and have
     suffered for my name,
and you have not grown weary.
Yet I hold this against you:
     you have lost the love you had at first.
Realize how far you have fallen.
Repent, and do the works you did at first.
Otherwise, I will come to you and remove
     your lampstand from its place,
unless you repent." ' "

The word of the Lord.

---

173. Rv 3:14-22

A reading from the Book of Revelation

Because you are lukewarm, neither hot nor cold,
I will spit you out of my mouth.

"To the angel of the Church in Laodicea,
     write this:
" 'The Amen, the faithful and true witness,
     the source of God's creation, says this:
     "I know your works;
     I know that you are neither cold nor hot.
I wish you were either cold or hot.
So, because you are lukewarm, neither hot
     nor cold,
     I will spit you out of my mouth.
For you say, 'I am rich and affluent and
     have no need of anything,'
     and yet do not realize that you are
          wretched,
     pitiable, poor, blind, and naked.
I advise you to buy from me gold refined
     by fire so that you may be rich,
     and white garments to put on
     so that your shameful nakedness may
          not be exposed,
     and buy ointment to smear on your eyes
          so that you may see.
Those whom I love, I reprove and chastise.
Be earnest, therefore, and repent.

" ' "Behold, I stand at the door and knock.
If anyone hears my voice and opens the
     door,
     then I will enter his house and dine with
          him,
     and he with me.
I will give the victor the right to sit with
     me on my throne,
     as I myself first won the victory
     and sit with my Father on his throne.
" ' "Whoever has ears ought to hear
     what the Spirit says to the churches." ' "

The word of the Lord.

---

174. Rv 20:11-15

A reading from the Book of Revelation

All the dead were judged according to their deeds.

Next I saw a large white throne and the
     one who was sitting on it.
The earth and the sky fled from his pres-
     ence
     and there was no place for them.
I saw the dead, the great and the lowly,
     standing before the throne,
     and scrolls were opened.
Then another scroll was opened, the book
     of life.
The dead were judged according to their
     deeds,
     by what was written in the scrolls.
The sea gave up its dead;
     then Death and Hades gave up their
          dead.
All the dead were judged according to
     their deeds.
Then Death and Hades were thrown into
     the pool of fire.
(This pool of fire is the second death.)
Anyone whose name was not found writ-
     ten in the book of life
     was thrown into the pool of fire.

The word of the Lord.

175. Rv 21:1-8

A reading from the Book of Revelation

The victor will inherit these gifts, and I shall be his God, and he will be my son.

I, John, saw a new heaven and a new earth.
The former heaven and the former earth had passed away,
  and the sea was no more.
I also saw the holy city, a new Jerusalem, coming down out of heaven from God,
  prepared as a bride adorned for her husband.
I heard a loud voice from the throne saying,
  "Behold, God's dwelling is with the human race.
He will dwell with them and they will be his people
  and God himself will always be with them as their God.
He will wipe every tear from their eyes,
  and there shall be no more death or mourning, wailing or pain,
  for the old order has passed away."

The one who sat on the throne said,
  "Behold, I make all things new."
Then he said, "Write these words down,
  for they are trustworthy and true."
He said to me, "They are accomplished.
I am the Alpha and the Omega,
  the beginning and the end.
To the thirsty I will give a gift
  from the spring of life-giving water.
The victor will inherit these gifts,
  and I shall be his God,
  and he will be my son.
But as for cowards, the unfaithful, the depraved,
  murderers, the unchaste, sorcerers, idol-worshipers,
  and deceivers of every sort,
  their lot is in the burning pool of fire and sulfur,
  which is the second death."

The word of the Lord.

READINGS FROM THE GOSPELS

176. Mt 3:1-12

✠ A reading from the holy Gospel
according to Matthew

Repent, for the Kingdom of heaven is at hand!

John the Baptist appeared, preaching in
the desert of Judea
and saying, "Repent, for the Kingdom of
heaven is at hand!"
It was of him that the prophet Isaiah had
spoken when he said:
A voice of one crying out in the desert,
Prepare the way of the Lord,
make straight his paths.
John wore clothing made of camel's hair
and had a leather belt around his
waist.
His food was locusts and wild honey.
At that time Jerusalem, all Judea,
and the whole region around the Jordan
were going out to him
and were being baptized by him in the
Jordan River
as they acknowledged their sins.

When he saw many of the Pharisees and
Sadducees
coming to his baptism, he said to them,
"You brood of vipers!
Who warned you to flee from the coming
wrath?
Produce good fruit as evidence of your re-
pentance.
And do not presume to say to yourselves,
'We have Abraham as our father.'
For I tell you,
God can raise up children to Abraham
from these stones.
Even now the ax lies at the root of the
trees.
Therefore every tree that does not bear
good fruit
will be cut down and thrown into the
fire.
I am baptizing you with water, for repen-
tance,
but the one who is coming after me is
mightier than I.
I am not worthy to carry his sandals.

He will baptize you with the Holy Spirit
and fire.
His winnowing fan is in his hand.
He will clear his threshing floor
and gather his wheat into his barn,
but the chaff he will burn with unquenchable fire."

The Gospel of the Lord.

177. Mt 4:12-17

✠ A reading from the holy Gospel
according to Matthew

Repent, for the Kingdom of heaven is at hand.

When Jesus heard that John had been arrested,
he withdrew to Galilee.
He left Nazareth and went to live in Capernaum by the sea,
in the region of Zebulun and Naphtali,
that what had been said through Isaiah
the prophet
might be fulfilled:
Land of Zebulun and land of Naphtali,
the way to the sea, beyond the Jor-
dan,
Galilee of the Gentiles,
the people who sit in darkness
have seen a great light,
on those dwelling in a land overshad-
owed by death
light has arisen.

From that time on, Jesus began to preach
and say,
"Repent, for the Kingdom of heaven is at
hand."

The Gospel of the Lord.

178. Mt 5:1-12

✠ A reading from the holy Gospel
according to Matthew

When Jesus saw the crowds, he went up the mountain,
and his disciples came to him.

When Jesus saw the crowds, he went up
the mountain,

and after he had sat down, his disciples came to him.

He began to teach them, saying:

"Blessed are the poor in spirit,
  for theirs is the Kingdom of heaven.
Blessed are they who mourn,
  for they will be comforted.
Blessed are the meek,
  for they will inherit the land.
Blessed are they who hunger and thirst
    for righteousness,
  for they will be satisfied.
Blessed are the merciful,
  for they will be shown mercy.
Blessed are the clean of heart,
  for they will see God.
Blessed are the peacemakers,
  for they will be called children of God.
Blessed are they who are persecuted for
    the sake of righteousness,
  for theirs is the Kingdom of heaven.
Blessed are you when they insult you and
    persecute you
  and utter every kind of evil against you
    falsely because of me.
Rejoice and be glad,
  for your reward will be great in heaven.
Thus they persecuted the prophets who
    were before you."

The Gospel of the Lord.

---

179. Mt 5:13-16

✠ A reading from the holy Gospel
    according to Matthew

Your light must shine before others.

Jesus said to his disciples:
"You are the salt of the earth.
But if salt loses its taste, with what can it
    be seasoned?
It is no longer good for anything
  but to be thrown out and trampled un-
    derfoot.
You are the light of the world.
A city set on a mountain cannot be hidden.
Nor do they light a lamp and then put it
    under a bushel basket;
  it is set on a lampstand,
  where it gives light to all in the house.

Just so, your light must shine before
    others,
  that they may see your good deeds
  and glorify your heavenly Father."

The Gospel of the Lord.

---

180. Mt 5:17-47

✠ A reading from the holy Gospel
    according to Matthew

But I say to you.

Jesus said to his disciples:
"Do not think that I have come to abol-
    ish the law or the prophets.
I have come not to abolish but to fulfill.
Amen, I say to you, until heaven and earth
    pass away,
  not the smallest letter or the smallest
    part of a letter
  will pass from the law,
  until all things have taken place.
Therefore, whoever breaks one of the least
    of these commandments
  and teaches others to do so
  will be called least in the Kingdom of
    heaven.
But whoever obeys and teaches these com-
    mandments
  will be called greatest in the Kingdom of
    heaven.
I tell you, unless your righteousness sur-
    passes
  that of the scribes and Pharisees,
  you will not enter the Kingdom of
    heaven.
"You have heard that it was said to your
    ancestors,
  *You shall not kill; and whoever kills will
    be liable to judgment.*
But I say to you,
  whoever is angry with brother
  will be liable to judgment;
  and whoever says to brother, *Raqa,*
  will be answerable to the Sanhedrin;
  and whoever says, 'You fool,'
  will be liable to fiery Gehenna.
Therefore, if you bring your gift to the
    altar,
  and there recall that your brother

has anything against you,
leave your gift there at the altar,
go first and be reconciled with your
brother,
and then come and offer your gift.
Settle with your opponent quickly while
on the way to court.
Otherwise your opponent will hand you
over to the judge,
and the judge will hand you over to the
guard,
and you will be thrown into prison.
Amen, I say to you,
you will not be released until you have
paid the last penny.
"You have heard that it was said,
You shall not commit adultery.
But I say to you,
everyone who looks at a woman with
lust
has already committed adultery with her
in his heart.
If your right eye causes you to sin,
tear it out and throw it away.
It is better for you to lose one of your
members
than to have your whole body thrown
into Gehenna.
And if your right hand causes you to sin,
cut it off and throw it away.
It is better for you to lose one of your
members
than to have your whole body go into
Gehenna.
"It was also said,
*Whoever divorces his wife must give her
a bill of divorce.*
But I say to you,
whoever divorces his wife—unless the
marriage is unlawful —
causes her to commit adultery,
and whoever marries a divorced woman
commits adultery.
"Again you have heard that it was said to
your ancestors,
Do not take a false oath,
*but make good to the Lord all that you
vow.*
But I say to you, do not swear at all;
not by heaven, for it is God's throne;

nor by the earth, for it is his footstool;
nor by Jerusalem, for it is the city of the
great King.
Do not swear by your head,
for you cannot make a single hair white
or black.
Let your 'Yes' mean 'Yes,' and your 'No'
mean 'No.'
Anything more is from the Evil One.
"You have heard that it was said,
*An eye for an eye and a tooth for a
tooth.*
But I say to you, offer no resistance to one
who is evil.
When someone strikes you on your right
cheek,
turn the other one as well.
If anyone wants to go to law with you over
your tunic,
hand over your cloak as well.
Should anyone press you into service for
one mile,
go for two miles.
Give to the one who asks of you,
and do not turn your back on one who
wants to borrow.
"You have heard that it was said,
*You shall love your neighbor and hate
your enemy.*
But I say to you, love your enemies
and pray for those who persecute you,
that you may be children of your heavenly Father,
for he makes his sun rise on the bad and
the good,
and causes rain to fall on the just and the
unjust.
For if you love those who love you, what
recompense will you have?
Do not the tax collectors do the same?
And if you greet your brothers only,
what is unusual about that?
Do not the pagans do the same?"

The Gospel of the Lord.

———————————————

181. Mt 9:1-8

✝ A reading from the holy Gospel
according to Matthew

Courage, child, your sins are forgiven.

After entering a boat, Jesus made the cross-
ing, and came into his own town.
And there people brought to him a paralytic
lying on a stretcher.
When Jesus saw their faith, he said to the
paralytic,
"Courage, child, your sins are forgiven."
At that, some of the scribes said to themselves,
"This man is blaspheming."
Jesus knew what they were thinking, and
said,
"Why do you harbor evil thoughts?
Which is easier, to say, 'Your sins are forgiven,'
or to say, 'Rise and walk'?
But that you may know that the Son of Man
has authority on earth to forgive sins"—
he then said to the paralytic,
"Rise, pick up your stretcher, and go
home."
He rose and went home.
When the crowds saw this they were struck
with awe
and glorified God who had given such authority to men.

The Gospel of the Lord.

182. Mt 9:9-13

✝ A reading from the holy Gospel
according to Matthew

I did not come to call the righteous but sinners.

As Jesus passed on from there,
he saw a man named Matthew sitting at
the customs post.
He said to him, "Follow me."
And he got up and followed him.
While he was at table in his house,
many tax collectors and sinners came
and sat with Jesus and his disciples.
The Pharisees saw this and said to his disciples,
"Why does your teacher eat with tax collectors and sinners?"

He heard this and said,
"Those who are well do not need a
physician, but the sick do.
Go and learn the meaning of the words,
I desire mercy, not sacrifice.
I did not come to call the righteous but sin-
ners."

The Gospel of the Lord.

183. Mt 18:15-20

✝ A reading from the holy Gospel
according to Matthew

You have won over your brother.

Jesus said to his disciples:
"If your brother sins against you,
go and tell him his fault between you and
him alone.
If he listens to you, you have won over your
brother.
If he does not listen,
take one or two others along with you,
so that every fact may be established
on the testimony of two or three witnesses.
If he refuses to listen to them, tell the
Church.
If he refuses to listen even to the Church,
then treat him as you would a Gentile or a
tax collector.
Amen, I say to you,
whatever you bind on earth shall be
bound in heaven,
and whatever you loose on earth shall be
loosed in heaven.
Again, amen, I say to you, if two of you
agree on earth
about anything for which they are to pray,
it shall be granted to them by my heavenly Father.
For where two or three are gathered together in my name,
there am I in the midst of them."

The Gospel of the Lord.

184. Mt 18:21-35

✢ **A reading from the holy Gospel according to Matthew**

So will my heavenly Father do to you,
unless each of you forgives your brother from your heart.

Peter approached Jesus and asked him,
 "Lord, if my brother sins against me,
 how often must I forgive him?
As many as seven times?"
Jesus answered, "I say to you, not seven
 times but seventy-seven times.
That is why the Kingdom of heaven may
 be likened to a king
 who decided to settle accounts with his
 servants.
When he began the accounting,
 a debtor was brought before him who
 owed him a huge amount.
Since he had no way of paying it back,
 his master ordered him to be sold,
 along with his wife, his children, and all
 his property,
 in payment of the debt.
At that, the servant fell down, did him
 homage, and said,
 'Be patient with me, and I will pay you
 back in full.'
Moved with compassion the master of that
 servant
 let him go and forgave him the loan.
When that servant had left, he found one
 of his fellow servants
 who owed him a much smaller amount.
He seized him and started to choke him,
 demanding,
 'Pay back what you owe.'
Falling to his knees, his fellow servant
 begged him,
 'Be patient with me, and I will pay you
 back.'
But he refused.
Instead, he had him put in prison
 until he paid back the debt.
Now when his fellow servants saw what
 had happened,
 they were deeply disturbed, and went to
 their master
 and reported the whole affair.
His master summoned him and said to
 him, 'You wicked servant!

I forgave you your entire debt because you
 begged me to.
Should you not have had pity on your fellow servant,
 as I had pity on you?'
Then in anger his master handed him over
 to the torturers
 until he should pay back the whole debt.
So will my heavenly Father do to you,
 unless each of you forgives your brother
 from your heart.'"

The Gospel of the Lord.

---

185. Mt 25:31-46

✢ **A reading from the holy Gospel according to Matthew**

Whatever you did for one of these least brothers of mine,
you did for me.

Jesus said to his disciples:
 "When the Son of Man comes in his glory,
 and all the angels with him,
 he will sit upon his glorious throne,
 and all the nations will be assembled before him.
And he will separate them one from another,
 as a shepherd separates the sheep from
 the goats.
He will place the sheep on his right and the
 goats on his left.
Then the king will say to those on his right,
 'Come, you who are blessed by my Father.
Inherit the kingdom prepared for you from
 the foundation of the world.
For I was hungry and you gave me food,
 I was thirsty and you gave me drink,
 a stranger and you welcomed me,
 naked and you clothed me,
 ill and you cared for me,
 in prison and you visited me.'
Then the righteous will answer him and say,
 'Lord, when did we see you hungry and
 feed you,
 or thirsty and give you drink?
When did we see you a stranger and welcome you,
 or naked and clothe you?
When did we see you ill or in prison, and
 visit you?'

And the king will say to them in reply,
  'Amen, I say to you, whatever you did
  for one of these least brothers of mine,
  you did for me.'
Then he will say to those on his left,
  'Depart from me, you accursed,
  into the eternal fire prepared for the Devil
  and his angels.
For I was hungry and you gave me no food,
  I was thirsty and you gave me no drink,
  a stranger and you gave me no welcome,
  naked and you gave me no clothing,
  ill and in prison, and you did not care for
  me.'
Then they will answer and say,
  'Lord, when did we see you hungry or
  thirsty
  or a stranger or naked or ill or in prison,
  and not minister to your needs?'
He will answer them, 'Amen, I say to you,
  what you did not do for one of these least
  ones,
  you did not do for me.'
And these will go off to eternal punishment,
  but the righteous to eternal life."

  The Gospel of the Lord.

---

186. Mt 26:69-75

✠ A reading from the holy Gospel
according to Matthew

He went out and began to weep bitterly.

Now Peter was sitting outside in the court-
  yard.
One of the maids came over to him and
  said,
  "You too were with Jesus the Galilean."
But he denied it in front of everyone, say-
  ing,
  "I do not know what you are talking
  about!"
As he went out to the gate, another girl
  saw him
  and said to those who were there,
  "This man was with Jesus the Naz-
  orean."
Again he denied it with an oath,
  "I do not know the man!"
A little later the bystanders came over and
  said to Peter,

"Surely you too are one of them;
  even your speech gives you away."
At that he began to curse and to swear,
  "I do not know the man."
And immediately a cock crowed.
Then Peter remembered the word that
  Jesus had spoken:
  "Before the cock crows you will deny me
  three times."
He went out and began to weep bitterly.

  The Gospel of the Lord.

---

187. Mk 12:28-34

✠ A reading from the holy Gospel
according to Mark

The first of all the commandments.

One of the scribes came to Jesus and asked
  him,
  "Which is the first of all the command-
  ments?"
Jesus replied, "The first is this:
  Hear, O Israel!
  The Lord our God is Lord alone!
You shall love the Lord your God with all
  your heart,
  with all your soul,
  with all your mind,
  and with all your strength.
The second is this:
  You shall love your neighbor as yourself.
There is no other commandment greater
  than these."
The scribe said to him, "Well said, teacher.
You are right in saying,
  He is One and there is no other than he.
And *to love him with all your heart,*
  with all your understanding,
  with all your strength,
  and to love your neighbor as yourself
  is worth more than all burnt offerings and
  sacrifices."
And when Jesus saw that he answered with
  understanding,
  he said to him,
  "You are not far from the Kingdom of
  God."
And no one dared to ask him any more
  questions.

  The Gospel of the Lord.

---

188. Lk 7:36-50

✠ A reading from the holy Gospel
according to Luke

But the one to whom little is forgiven, loves little.

A certain Pharisee invited Jesus to dine
with him,
    and he entered the Pharisee's house and
    reclined at table.
Now there was a sinful woman in the city
    who learned that he was at table in the
    house of the Pharisee.
Bringing an alabaster flask of ointment,
    she stood behind him at his feet weeping
    and began to bathe his feet with her
    tears.
Then she wiped them with her hair,
    kissed them, and anointed them with the
    ointment.
When the Pharisee who had invited him
    saw this he said to himself,
    "If this man were a prophet,
    he would know who and what sort of
    woman this is who is touching him,
    that she is a sinner."
Jesus said to him in reply,
    "Simon, I have something to say to you."
"Tell me, teacher," he said.
"Two people were in debt to a certain
    creditor;
    one owed five hundred days' wages and
    the other owed fifty.
Since they were unable to repay the debt,
    he forgave it for both.
Which of them will love him more?"
Simon said in reply,
    "The one, I suppose, whose larger debt
    was forgiven."
He said to him, "You have judged rightly."
Then he turned to the woman and said to
    Simon,
    "Do you see this woman?
When I entered your house, you did not
    give me water for my feet,
    but she has bathed them with her tears
    and wiped them with her hair.
You did not give me a kiss,
    but she has not ceased kissing my feet
    since the time I entered.
You did not anoint my head with oil,
    but she anointed my feet with ointment.

So I tell you, her many sins have been for-
    given;
    hence, she has shown great love.
But the one to whom little is forgiven,
    loves little."
He said to her, "Your sins are forgiven."
The others at table said to themselves,
    "Who is this who even forgives sins?"
But he said to the woman,
    "Your faith has saved you; go in peace."

The Gospel of the Lord.

———————————

189. Lk 13:1-5

✠ A reading from the holy Gospel
according to Luke

If you do not repent, you will all perish as they did!

Some people told Jesus about the Gali-
    leans
    whose blood Pilate had mingled with the
    blood of their sacrifices.
He said to them in reply,
    "Do you think that because these Gali-
    leans suffered in this way
    they were greater sinners than all other
    Galileans?
By no means!
But I tell you, if you do not repent,
    you will all perish as they did!
Or those eighteen people who were killed
    when the tower at Siloam fell on them—
    do you think they were more guilty
    than everyone else who lived in Jerusa-
    lem?
By no means!
But I tell you, if you do not repent,
    you will all perish as they did!"

The Gospel of the Lord.

———————————

190. Lk 15:1-10

✛ A reading from the holy Gospel according to Luke

There will be more joy in heaven
over one sinner who repents.

The tax collectors and sinners were all
drawing near to listen to Jesus,
but the Pharisees and scribes began to
complain, saying,
"This man welcomes sinners and eats
with them."
So Jesus addressed this parable to them.
"What man among you having a hundred
sheep and losing one of them
would not leave the ninety-nine in the
desert
and go after the lost one until he finds it?
And when he does find it,
he sets it on his shoulders with great joy
and, upon his arrival home,
he calls together his friends and neighbors and says to them,
'Rejoice with me because I have found
my lost sheep.'
I tell you, in just the same way
there will be more joy in heaven over
one sinner who repents
than over ninety-nine righteous people
who have no need of repentance.

"Or what woman having ten coins and losing one
would not light a lamp and sweep the
house,
searching carefully until she finds it?
And when she does find it,
she calls together her friends and neighbors
and says to them,
'Rejoice with me because I have found
the coin that I lost.'
In just the same way, I tell you,
there will be rejoicing among the angels
of God
over one sinner who repents."

The Gospel of the Lord.

---

191. Lk 15:1-3, 11-32

✛ A reading from the holy Gospel according to Luke

While he was still a long way off,
his father caught sight of him, and was filled with compassion.

Jesus addressed this parable to them.
"A man had two sons, and the younger son
said to his father,
'Father, give me the share of your estate
that should come to me.'
So the father divided the property between
them.
After a few days, the younger son collected all his belongings
and set off to a distant country
where he squandered his inheritance on
a life of dissipation.
When he had freely spent everything,
a severe famine struck that country,
and he found himself in dire need.
So he hired himself out to one of the local
citizens
who sent him to his farm to tend the
swine.
And he longed to eat his fill of the pods on
which the swine fed,
but nobody gave him any.
Coming to his senses he thought,
'How many of my father's hired workers
have more than enough food to eat,
but here am I, dying from hunger.
I shall get up and go to my father and I
shall say to him,
"Father, I have sinned against heaven
and against you.
I no longer deserve to be called your son;
treat me as you would treat one of your
hired workers." '
So he got up and went back to his father.
While he was still a long way off,
his father caught sight of him, and was
filled with compassion.
He ran to his son, embraced him and
kissed him.
His son said to him,
'Father, I have sinned against heaven
and against you;
I no longer deserve to be called your
son.'

But his father ordered his servants,
  'Quickly, bring the finest robe and put it
    on him;
  put a ring on his finger and sandals on
    his feet.
Take the fattened calf and slaughter it.
Then let us celebrate with a feast,
  because this son of mine was dead, and
    has come to life again;
  he was lost, and has been found.'
Then the celebration began.
Now the older son had been out in the field
  and, on his way back, as he neared the
    house,
  he heard the sound of music and danc-
    ing.
He called one of the servants and asked
    what this might mean.
The servant said to him,
  'Your brother has returned
  and your father has slaughtered the fat-
    tened calf
  because he has him back safe and
    sound.'
He became angry,
  and when he refused to enter the house,
  his father came out and pleaded with
    him.
He said to his father in reply,
  'Look, all these years I served you
  and not once did I disobey your orders;
  yet you never gave me even a young
    goat to feast on with my friends.
But when your son returns
  who swallowed up your property with
    prostitutes,
  for him you slaughter the fattened calf.'
He said to him,
  'My son, you are here with me always;
  everything I have is yours.
But now we must celebrate and rejoice,
  because your brother was dead and has
    come to life again;
  he was lost and has been found.' "
          The Gospel of the Lord.

---

192. Lk 17:1-4

✠ A reading from the holy Gospel
        according to Luke

*If your brother wrongs you seven times in one day
and returns to you seven times saying, "I am sorry,"
you should forgive him.*

Jesus said to his disciples,
  "Things that cause sin will inevitably
    occur,
  but woe to the one through whom they
    occur.
It would be better for him if a millstone
    were put around his neck
  and he be thrown into the sea
  than for him to cause one of these little
    ones to sin.
Be on your guard!
If your brother sins, rebuke him;
  and if he repents, forgive him.
And if he wrongs you seven times in one
    day
  and returns to you seven times saying, 'I
    am sorry,'
  you should forgive him."
          The Gospel of the Lord.

---

193. Lk 18:9-14

✠ A reading from the holy Gospel
        according to Luke

O God, be merciful to me a sinner.

Jesus addressed this parable
  to those who were convinced of their
    own righteousness
  and despised everyone else.
"Two people went up to the temple area to
    pray;
  one was a Pharisee and the other was a
    tax collector.
The Pharisee took up his position and
    spoke this prayer to himself,
  'O God, I thank you that I am not like the
    rest of humanity—
  greedy, dishonest, adulterous—or even
    like this tax collector.
I fast twice a week,
  and I pay tithes on my whole income.'
But the tax collector stood off at a distance
  and would not even raise his eyes to
    heaven

but beat his breast and prayed,
   'O God, be merciful to me a sinner.'
I tell you, the latter went home justified,
   not the former;
   for everyone who exalts himself will be
      humbled,
   and the one who humbles himself will be
      exalted."

The Gospel of the Lord.

194. Lk 19:1-10

✠ A reading from the holy Gospel
according to Luke

The Son of Man has come to seek
and to save what was lost.

At that time Jesus came to Jericho and in-
   tended to pass through the town.
Now a man there named Zacchaeus,
   who was a chief tax collector and also a
      wealthy man,
   was seeking to see who Jesus was;
   but he could not see him because of the
      crowd,
   for he was short in stature.
So he ran ahead and climbed a sycamore
   tree in order to see Jesus,
   who was about to pass that way.
When he reached the place, Jesus looked
   up and said,
   "Zacchaeus, come down quickly,
   for today I must stay at your house."
And he came down quickly and received
   him with joy.
When they saw this, they began to grum-
   ble, saying,
   "He has gone to stay at the house of a
      sinner."
But Zacchaeus stood there and said to the
   Lord,
   "Behold, half of my possessions, Lord, I
      shall give to the poor,
   and if I have extorted anything from
      anyone
   I shall repay it four times over."
And Jesus said to him,
   "Today salvation has come to this house
   because this man too is a descendant of
      Abraham.

For the Son of Man has come to seek
   and to save what was lost."

The Gospel of the Lord.

195. Lk 23:39-43

✠ A reading from the holy Gospel
according to Luke

Today you will be with me in Paradise.

One of the criminals hanging in crucifixion
   reviled Jesus, saying,
   "Are you not the Christ?
   Save yourself and us."
The other man however, rebuking him,
   said in reply,
   "Have you no fear of God,
   for you are subject to the same condem-
      nation?
And indeed, we have been condemned
   justly,
   for the sentence we received corre-
      sponds to our crimes,
   but he has done nothing criminal."
Then he said,
   "Jesus, remember me when you come
      into your Kingdom."
He replied to him,
   "Amen, I say to you,
   today you will be with me in Paradise."

The Gospel of the Lord.

196. Jn 8:1-11

✠ A reading from the holy Gospel
according to John

Go, and from now on do not sin any more.

Jesus went to the Mount of Olives.
But early in the morning he arrived again
   in the temple area,
   and all the people started coming to him,
   and he sat down and taught them.
Then the scribes and the Pharisees brought
   a woman
   who had been caught in adultery
   and made her stand in the middle.
They said to him,
   "Teacher, this woman was caught
   in the very act of committing adultery.
Now in the law, Moses commanded us to
   stone such women.

So what do you say?"
They said this to test him,
  so that they could have some charge to
    bring against him.
Jesus bent down and began to write on the
    ground with his finger.
But when they continued asking him,
  he straightened up and said to them,
  "Let the one among you who is without
    sin
  be the first to throw a stone at her."
Again he bent down and wrote on the
    ground.
And in response, they went away one by
    one,
  beginning with the elders.
So he was left alone with the woman before
    him.
Then Jesus straightened up and said to her,
  "Woman, where are they?
Has no one condemned you?"
She replied, "No one, sir."
Then Jesus said, "Neither do I condemn
    you.
Go, and from now on do not sin any more."
    The Gospel of the Lord.

---

197. Jn 8:31-36

✠ A reading from the holy Gospel
according to John

Everyone who commits sin is a slave of sin.

Jesus said to those Jews who believed in
    him,
  "If you remain in my word, you will truly
    be my disciples,
  and you will know the truth, and the truth
    will set you free."
They answered him, "We are descendants
    of Abraham
  and have never been enslaved to anyone.
How can you say, 'You will become free'?"
Jesus answered them, "Amen, amen, I say
    to you,
  everyone who commits sin is a slave of
    sin.
A slave does not remain in a household for-
    ever,
  but a son always remains.

So if the Son frees you, then you will truly
    be free."
    The Gospel of the Lord.

---

198. Jn 15:1-8

✠ A reading from the holy Gospel
according to John

*He takes away every branch in me that does not bear fruit,
and everyone that does he prunes so that it bears more fruit.*

Jesus said to his disciples:
"I am the true vine, and my Father is the
    vine grower.
He takes away every branch in me that does
    not bear fruit,
  and everyone that does he prunes so that
    it bears more fruit.
You are already pruned because of the word
    that I spoke to you.
Remain in me, as I remain in you.
Just as a branch cannot bear fruit on its
    own
  unless it remains on the vine,
  so neither can you unless you remain in
    me.
I am the vine, you are the branches.
Whoever remains in me and I in him will
    bear much fruit,
  because without me you can do nothing.
Anyone who does not remain in me
  will be thrown out like a branch and
    wither;
  people will gather them and throw them
    into a fire
  and they will be burned.
If you remain in me and my words remain in
    you,
  ask for whatever you want and it will be
    done for you.
By this is my Father glorified,
  that you bear much fruit and become my
    disciples."
    The Gospel of the Lord.

---

199. Jn 15:9-14

✛ A reading from the holy Gospel
according to John

You are my friends if you do what I command you.

Jesus said to his disciples:
"As the Father loves me, so I also love you.
Remain in my love.
If you keep my commandments, you will
   remain in my love,
   just as I have kept my Father's commandments
   and remain in his love.

"I have told you this so that my joy might
   be in you
   and your joy might be complete.
This is my commandment: love one another as I love you.
No one has greater love than this,
   to lay down one's life for one's friends.
You are my friends if you do what I command you."

The Gospel of the Lord.

---

200. Jn 19:13-37

✛ A reading from the holy Gospel
according to John

They will look upon him whom they have pierced.

When Pilate heard these words he brought
   Jesus out
   and seated him on the judge's bench
   in the place called Stone Pavement, in
   Hebrew, Gabbatha.
It was preparation day for Passover, and it
   was about noon.
And he said to the Jews,
   "Behold, your king!"
They cried out,
   "Take him away, take him away! Cru-
   cify him!"
Pilate said to them,
   "Shall I crucify your king?"
The chief priests answered,
   "We have no king but Caesar."
Then he handed him over to them to be
   crucified.

So they took Jesus, and, carrying the cross
   himself,

he went out to what is called the Place of
   the Skull,
   in Hebrew, Golgotha.
There they crucified him, and with him
   two others,
   one on either side, with Jesus in the middle.
Pilate also had an inscription written and
   put on the cross.
It read,
   "Jesus the Nazorean, the King of the
   Jews."
Now many of the Jews read this inscription,
   because the place where Jesus was crucified was near the city;
   and it was written in Hebrew, Latin, and
   Greek.
So the chief priests of the Jews said to Pilate,
   "Do not write 'The King of the Jews,'
   but that he said, 'I am the King of the
   Jews.' "
Pilate answered,
   "What I have written, I have written."
When the soldiers had crucified Jesus,
   they took his clothes and divided them
   into four shares,
   a share for each soldier.
They also took his tunic, but the tunic was
   seamless,
   woven in one piece from the top down.
So they said to one another,
   "Let's not tear it, but cast lots for it to
   see whose it will be,"
   in order that the passage of Scripture
   might be fulfilled that says:
      They divided my garments among them,
      and for my vesture they cast lots.
This is what the soldiers did.
Standing by the cross of Jesus were his
   mother
   and his mother's sister, Mary the wife of
   Clopas,
   and Mary Magdalene.
When Jesus saw his mother and the disciple there whom he loved
   he said to his mother, "Woman, behold,
   your son."
Then he said to the disciple,
   "Behold, your mother."

And from that hour the disciple took her into his home.

After this, aware that everything was now finished,

in order that the Scripture might be fulfilled,

Jesus said, "I thirst."

There was a vessel filled with common wine.

So they put a sponge soaked in wine on a sprig of hyssop

and put it up to his mouth.

When Jesus had taken the wine, he said, "It is finished."

And bowing his head, he handed over the spirit.

Now since it was preparation day,

in order that the bodies might not remain on the cross on the sabbath,

for the sabbath day of that week was a solemn one,

the Jews asked Pilate that their legs be broken

and that they be taken down.

So the soldiers came and broke the legs of the first

and then of the other one who was crucified with Jesus.

But when they came to Jesus and saw that he was already dead,

they did not break his legs,

but one soldier thrust his lance into his side,

and immediately Blood and water flowed out.

An eyewitness has testified, and his testimony is true;

he knows that he is speaking the truth,

so that you also may come to believe.

For this happened so that the Scripture passage might be fulfilled:

Not a bone of it will be broken.

And again another passage says:

They will look upon him whom they have pierced.

The Gospel of the Lord.

---

201. Jn 20:19-23

✠ A reading from the holy Gospel according to John

Receive the Holy Spirit.
Whose sins you forgive are forgiven them.

On the evening of that first day of the week,

when the doors were locked, where the disciples were,

for fear of the Jews,

Jesus came and stood in their midst

and said to them, "Peace be with you."

When he had said this, he showed them his hands and his side.

The disciples rejoiced when they saw the Lord.

Jesus said to them again, "Peace be with you.

As the Father has sent me, so I send you."

And when he had said this, he breathed on them and said to them,

"Receive the Holy Spirit.

Whose sins you forgive are forgiven them,

and whose sins you retain are retained."

The Gospel of the Lord.

INVITATION OF THE MINISTER FOR THE GENERAL CONFESSION OF SINS

202. If the prayer is directed to the Father:

1

Dear friends in Christ, our merciful Father does not desire the death of the sinner but rather that he should turn back to him and have life. Let us pray that we who are sorry for our past sins may fear no future evil and sin no more.

℞. Spare us, Lord; spare your people.

2

God who is infinitely merciful pardons all who are repentant and takes away their guilt. Confident in his goodness, let us ask him to forgive all our sins as we confess them with sincerity of heart.

℞. Lord, hear our prayer.

3

God gave us his Son for our sins and raised him up to make us holy. Let us humbly pray to the Father.

℞. Lord, have mercy on your people.

4

God our Father waits for the return of those who are lost and welcomes them back as his children. Let us pray that we may turn back to him and be received with kindness into his house.

℞. Lord, do not hold our sins against us.

OR:

> Father, we have sinned in your sight; we are unworthy to be called your children.

5

Our God seeks out what is lost, leads home the abandoned, binds up what is broken and gives strength to the weak; let us ask him to help us.

R̦. Lord, heal our weakness.

203.

1

Jesus Christ is the victor over life and death: in his mercy may he pardon our offenses against God and reconcile us with the Church we have wounded by our sins.

R̦. Lord Jesus, be our salvation.

2

In his great love Christ willingly suffered and died for our sins and for the sins of all mankind. Let us come before him with faith and hope to pray for the salvation of the world.

R̦. Christ, graciously hear us.

3

Let us pray with confidence to Christ, the Good Shepherd, who seeks out the lost sheep and carries it back with joy.

R̦. Lord, seek us out and bring us home.

4

Christ our Lord bore our sins upon the cross and by his suffering has brought us healing, so that we live for God and are dead to sin. Let us pray with humility and trust.

℟. Lord, to whom shall we go? You have the words of eternal life. We have come to believe and to know that you are the Christ, the Son of God.

OR:

Have pity on us, and help us.

5

Christ our Lord was given up to death for our sins and rose again for our justification. Let us pray to him with confidence in his goodness.

℟. You are our Savior.

OR:

Jesus Christ, Son of the living God, have pity on us.

PENITENTIAL INTERCESSIONS

(At least one of the intercessions should always be a petition for a true conversion of heart.)

204. If the prayer is addressed to the Father:

1

—By human weakness we have disfigured the holiness of the Church: pardon all our sins and restore us to full communion with our brethren.

℟. Lord, hear our prayer.

OR:

Lord, hear us.

Or another suitable response may be used.

—Your mercy is our hope: welcome us to the sacrament of reconciliation. ℟.

—Give us the will to change our lives, and the lives of others, by charity, good example and prayer. ℟.

—As we make our confession, rescue us from slavery to sin and lead us to the freedom enjoyed by your children. ℟.

—Make us a living sign of your love for all to see: people reconciled with you and with each other. ℟.

—Through the sacrament of reconciliation may we grow in your peace and seek to spread it throughout the world. ℟.

—In this sign of your love you forgive us our sills: may it teach us to love others and to forgive their sins against us. ℟.

—In your mercy clothe us in the wedding garment of grace and welcome us to your table. ℟.

—Forgive us our sins, lead us in the ways of goodness and love, and bring us to the reward of everlasting peace. ℟.

—Give light to our darkness and lead us by your truth. ℟.

—In justice you punish us: in your mercy set us free for the glory of your name. ℟.

—May your power keep safe from all danger those whom your love sets free from the chains of sin. ℟.

—Look on our weakness: do not be angry and condemn, but in your love cleanse, guide and save us. ℟.

—In your mercy free us from the past and enable us to begin a new life of holiness. ℟.

—When we stray from you, guide us back into the way of holiness, love and peace. ℟.

—By your redeeming love overcome our sinfulness and the harm it has brought us. ℟.

—Blot out the sins of the past and fit us for the life that is to come. ℟.

2

The following intercessions may be used with a variable response or with an invariable response as in the "Liturgy of the Hours."

In your goodness forgive our sins against the unity of your family,
—make us one in heart, one in spirit.

We have sinned, Lord, we have sinned,
—take away our sins by your saving grace.

Give us pardon for our sins,
—and reconciliation with your Church.

Touch our hearts and change our lives, make us grow always in your friendship,
—help us to make up for our sins against your wisdom and goodness.

Cleanse and renew your Church, Lord,
—may it grow in strength as a witness to you.

Touch the hearts of those who have abandoned you through sin and scandal,
—call them back to you and keep them faithful in your love.

May we show forth in our lives the sufferings of your Son,
—you raised us up to life when you raised him from the dead.

Have mercy on us, Lord, as we praise and thank you,
—with your pardon give us also your peace.

Lord, our sins are many, but we trust in your mercy,
—call us, and we shall turn to you.

Receive us as we come before you with humble and contrite hearts,
—those who trust in you shall never trust in vain.

We have turned away from you and fallen into sin,
—we have followed evil ways and rejected your commandments.

Turn to us, Lord, and show us your mercy; blot out our sins,
—cast them into the depths of the sea.

Restore us, Lord, to your favor, and give us joy in your presence,
—may our glory be to serve you with all our hearts.

205. If the prayer is addressed to Christ:

1

—By your death you reconciled us with the Father and brought us salvation.   (Romans 5:10)

℟.   Lord, have mercy.

OR:

Christ, hear us.

Or another suitable response may be used.

—You died and rose again, and sit at the right hand of the Father, to make intercession for us. ℟.   (Romans 8:34)

—You came from God as our wisdom and justice, our sanctification and redemption. ℟.   (1 Corinthians 1:30)

—You washed mankind in the Spirit of our God: you made us holy and righteous. ℟.   (1 Corinthians 6:11)

—You warned us that if we sin against each other we sin against you. ℟.   (1 Corinthians 8:12)

—Though you were rich you became poor for our sake, so that by your poverty we might become rich. ℟.   (2 Corinthians 8:9)

—You gave yourself up for our sins to save us from this evil world. ℟.   (Galatians 1:4)

—You rose from the dead to save us from the anger that was to come. ℟.   (1 Thessalonians 1:10)

—You came into the world to save sinners. ℟.   (1 Timothy 1:15)

—You gave yourself up to bring redemption to all. ℟.
                                                          (1 Timothy 2:6)

—You destroyed death and gave light to life. ℟.   (2 Timothy 1:10)

—You will come to judge the living and the dead. ℟.
                                                          (2 Timothy 4:1)

—You gave yourself up for us to redeem us from all sin and to prepare for yourself a holy people, marked as your own, devoted to good works. ℟.   (Titus 2:14)

—You showed us your mercy, and as a faithful high priest in the things of God you made atonement for the sins of the people. ℟.   (Hebrews 2:17)

—You became the source of salvation for all who obey you. ℟.
                                                          (Hebrews 5:9)

—Through the Holy Spirit you offered yourself to God as a spotless victim, cleansing our consciences from lifeless works. ℟.   (Hebrews 9:15)

—You were offered in sacrifice to undo the sins of the many. ℟.
                                                          (Hebrews 9:28)

—Once and for all you died for our sins, the innocent one for the guilty. ℟.   (1 Peter 3:18)

—You are the atonement for our sins and for the sins of the world. ℟.   (1 John 2:2)

—You died that those who believe in you may not perish but have eternal life. ℟.   (John 3:16, 35)

—You came into the world to seek and save what was lost. ℟.   (Matthew 18:11)

—You were sent by the Father, not to judge the world but to save it. ℟.   (John 3:17)

—You have power on earth to forgive sins. ℟.   (Mark 2:10)

—You invite all who labor and are burdened to come to you to be refreshed. ℟.   (Matthew 11:28)

—You gave your apostles the keys of the kingdom of heaven, the power to bind and to loose. ℟.   (Matthew 16:19; 18:18)

—You told us that the whole law depends on love of God and of our neighbor. ℟.   (Matthew 22:38-40)

—Jesus, life of all mankind, you came into the world to give us life, life in its fullness. ℟.   (John 10:10)

—Jesus, God Shepherd, you gave your life for your sheep. ℟.   (John 10:11)

—Jesus, eternal truth, you give us true freedom. ℟.   (John 14:6; 8:32, 36)

—Jesus, you are the way to the Father, ℞.   (John 14:6)

—Jesus, you are the resurrection and life; those who believe in you, even if they are dead, will live. ℞.   (John 11:25)

—Jesus, true vine, the Father prunes your branches to make them bear even greater fruit. ℞.   (John 15:1-2)

2

The following intercessions may be used with a variable response or with an invariable response as in the "Liturgy of the Hours."

Healer of body and soul, bind up the wounds of our hearts,
—that our lives may grow strong through grace.

Help us to strip ourselves of sin,
—and put on the new life of grace.

Redeemer of the world, give us the spirit of penance and a deeper devotion to your passion,
—so that we may have a fuller share in your risen glory.

May your Mother, the refuge of sinners, intercede for us,
—and ask you in your goodness to pardon our sins.

You forgave the woman who repented,
—show us also your mercy.

You brought back the lost sheep on your shoulders,
—pity us and lead us home.

You promised Paradise to the good thief,
—take us with you into your Kingdom.

You died for us and rose again,
—make us share in your death and resurrection.

PROCLAMATION OF PRAISE

206.

1   Psalm 32:1-2, 3-4, 5, 6, 7, 10-11

℟.   Let the just exult and rejoice in the Lord.

**Blessed is he whose fault is taken away,
     whose sin is covered.
Blessed the man to whom the L**ORD** imputes not guilt
     in whose spirit there is no guile.**

℟.   Let the just exult and rejoice in the Lord.

**As long as I would not speak, my bones wasted away
     with my groaning all the day,
For day and night your hand was heavy upon me;
     my strength was dried up as by the heat of summer.**

℟.   Let the just exult and rejoice in the Lord.

**Then I acknowledged my sin to you,
     my guilt I covered not.
I said, "I confess my faults to the L**ORD**,"
     and you took away the guilt of my sin.**

℟.   Let the just exult and rejoice in the Lord.

**For this shall every faithful man pray to you
     in time of stress.
Though deep waters overflow,
     they shall not reach him.**

℟.   Let the just exult and rejoice in the Lord.

**You are my shelter; from distress you will preserve me;
     with glad cries of freedom you will ring me round.**

℟.   Let the just exult and rejoice in the Lord.

**Many are the sorrows of the wicked,
     but mercy surrounds him who trusts in the L**ORD**.**

Be glad in the LORD **and rejoice, you just;**
  exult all you upright of heart.

  ℟.   Let the just exult and rejoice in the Lord.

2   Psalm 98:1, 2-3a, 3b-4, 5-6, 7-8, 9

  ℟.   The Lord has remembered his mercy.

Sing to the LORD **a new song,**
  for he has done wondrous deeds;
His right hand has won victory for him,
  his holy arm.

  ℟.   The Lord has remembered his mercy.

The LORD **has made his salvation known:**
  in the sight of the nations he has revealed his justice.
He has remembered his mercy and his faithfulness
  toward the house of Israel.

  ℟.   The Lord has remembered his mercy.

All the ends of the earth have seen
  the salvation by our God.
Sing joyfully to the LORD**, all you lands;**
  break into song; sing praise.

  ℟.   The Lord has remembered his mercy.

Sing praise to the LORD **with the harp,**
  with the harp and melodious song.
With trumpets and the sound of the horn
  sing joyfully before the King, the LORD**.**

  ℟.   The Lord has remembered his mercy.

Let the sea and what fills it resound,
  the world and those who dwell in it;
Let the rivers clap their hands.
  the mountains shout with them for joy.

℞.   The Lord has remembered his mercy.

Before the LORD, for he comes,
   for he comes to rule the earth;
He will rule the world with justice
   and the peoples with equity.

℞.   The Lord has remembered his mercy.

3   Psalm 100:1b-2, 3, 4, 5

℞.   The Lord is loving and kind: his mercy is for ever.

Sing joyfully to the LORD, all you lands;
   serve the LORD with gladness;
   come before him with joyful song.

℞.   The Lord is loving and kind: his mercy is for ever.

Know that the LORD is God;
   he made us, his we are;
   his people, the flock he tends.

℞.   The Lord is loving and kind: his mercy is for ever.

Enter his gates with thanksgiving,
   his courts with praise;
Give thanks to him; bless his name.

℞.   The Lord is loving and kind: his mercy is for ever.

The LORD is good:
   the LORD, whose kindness endures forever,
   and his faithfulness, to all generations.

℞.   The Lord is loving and kind: his mercy is for ever.

4   Psalm 119:1, 10-11, 12-13, 15-16, 18 and 33, 105, 169-170, 174-175

℞.   Blessed are you, Lord; teach me your decrees.

Blessed are they whose way is blameless.
  who walk in the law of the LORD.

  ℟.   Blessed are you, Lord; teach me your decrees.

With all my heart I seek you;
  let me not stray from your commands.
Within my heart I treasure your promise,
  that I may not sin against you.

  ℟.   Blessed are you, Lord; teach me your decrees.

Blessed are you, O LORD;
  teach me your statutes.
With my lips I declare
  all the ordinances of your mouth.

  ℟.   Blessed are you, Lord; teach me your decrees.

I will meditate on your precepts
  and consider your ways.
In your statutes I will delight;
  I will not forget your words.

  ℟.   Blessed are you, Lord; teach me your decrees.

Open my eyes, that I may consider
  the wonders of your law.
Instruct me, O LORD, in the way of your statutes,
  that I may exactly observe them.

  ℟.   Blessed are you, Lord; teach me your decrees.

A lamp to my feet is your word,
  a light to my path.

  ℟.   Blessed are you, Lord; teach me your decrees.

Let my cry come before you, O LORD;
  in keeping with your word, give me discernment.
Let my supplication reach you;
  rescue me according to your promise.

℟.   Blessed are you, Lord; teach me your decrees.

I long for your salvation, O LORD,
and your law is my delight.
Let my soul live to praise you,
and may your ordinances help me.

℟.   Blessed are you, Lord; teach me your decrees.

5   Psalm 103:1-2, 3-4, 8-9, 10-11, 12-13, 14-15, 16-18

℟.   The Lord's kindness is everlasting to those who fear
him.

Bless the LORD, O my soul;
and all my being, bless his holy name.
Bless the LORD, O my soul,
and forget not all his benefits.

℟.   The Lord's kindness is everlasting to those who fear
him.

He pardons all your iniquities,
he heals all your ills.
He redeems your life from destruction,
he crowns you with kindness and compassion.

℟.   The Lord's kindness is everlasting to those who fear
him.

Merciful and gracious is the LORD,
slow to anger and abounding in kindness.
He will not always chide,
nor does he keep his wrath forever.

℟.   The Lord's kindness is everlasting to those who fear
him.

Not according to our sins does he deal with us,
nor does he requite us according to our crimes.

For as the heavens are high above the earth,
    so surpassing is his mercy toward those who fear him.

    ℟.   The Lord's kindness is everlasting to those who fear
        him.

As a father has compassion on his children,
    so the LORD has compassion on those who fear him.
For he knows how we are formed;
    he remembers that we are dust.

    ℟.   The Lord's kindness is everlasting to those who fear
        him.

Man's days are like those of grass;
    like a flower of the field he blooms.
The wind sweeps over him and he is gone,
    and his place knows him no more.

    ℟.   The Lord's kindness is everlasting to those who fear
        him.

But the mercy of the LORD is from eternity
    to eternity toward those who fear him.
And his justice toward children's children
    among those who keep his covenant
    and remember to fulfill his precepts.

    ℟.   The Lord's kindness is everlasting to those who fear
        him.

6   Psalm 145:1-2, 3-4, 5-7, 8-9, 10-11, 12-13a,
                                       13b-14, 15-16, 17-18, 19-20, 21

    ℟.   Day after day I will bless you, Lord; I will praise
        your name for ever.

I will extol you, O my God and King,
    and I will bless your name forever and ever.
Every day will I bless you,
    and I will praise your name forever and ever.

℞. Day after day I will bless you, Lord; I will praise your name for ever.

Great is the LORD and highly to be praised;
his greatness is unsearchable.
Generation after generation praises your works
and proclaims your might.

℞. Day after day I will bless you, Lord; I will praise your name for ever.

They speak of the splendor of your majesty
and tell of your wondrous works.
They discourse of the power of your terrible deeds
and declare your greatness.
They publish the fame of your abundant goodness
and joyfully sing of your justice.

℞. Day after day I will bless you, Lord; I will praise your name for ever.

The LORD is gracious and merciful,
slow to anger and of great mercy.
The LORD is good to all
and compassionate toward all his works.

℞. Day after day I will bless you, Lord; I will praise your name for ever.

Let all your works give you thanks, O LORD,
and let your faithful ones bless you.
Let them discourse of the glory of your Kingdom
and speak of your might.

℞. Day after day I will bless you, Lord; I will praise your name for ever.

Making known to men your might
and the glorious splendor of your Kingdom.
Your Kingdom is a Kingdom for all ages,
and your dominion endures through all generations.

℟. Day after day I will bless you, Lord; I will praise your name for ever.

The LORD is faithful in all his words
    and holy in all his works.
The LORD lifts up all who are falling
    and raises up all who are bowed down.

℟. Day after day I will bless you, Lord; I will praise your name for ever.

The eyes of all look hopefully to you,
    and you give them food in due season;
You open your hand
    and satisfy the desire of every living thing.

℟. Day after day I will bless you, Lord; I will praise your name for ever.

The LORD is just in all his ways
    and holy in all his works.
The LORD is near to all who call upon him
    to all who call upon him in truth.

℟. Day after day I will bless you, Lord; I will praise your name for ever.

He fulfills the desire of those who fear him,
    he hears their cry and saves them.
The LORD keeps all who love him,
    but all the wicked he will destroy.

℟. Day after day I will bless you, Lord; I will praise your name for ever.

May my mouth speak the praise of the LORD,
    and may all flesh bless his holy name
    forever and ever.

℟. Day after day I will bless you, Lord; I will praise your name for ever.

7 Psalm 146:1b-2, 3-4, 5-6b, 6c-7a, 7b-8, 9-10

℟. I will sing to my God all the days of my life.

Praise the Lord, O my soul;
I will praise the LORD all my life;
I will sing praise to my God while I live.

℟. I will sing to my God all the days of my life.

Put not your trust in princes,
in man, in whom there is no salvation.
When his spirit departs, he returns to the earth;
on that day his plans perish.

℟. I will sing to my God all the days of my life.

Blessed he whose help is the God of Jacob,
whose hope is in the LORD, his God.
Who made heaven and earth,
the sea and all that is in them.

℟. I will sing to my God all the days of my life.

The LORD keeps faith forever,
secures justice for the oppressed,
gives food to the hungry.

℟. I will sing to my God all the days of my life.

The LORD sets captives free;
the LORD gives sight to the blind.
The LORD raises up those that were bowed down;
the LORD loves the just.

℟. I will sing to my God all the days of my life.

The LORD protects strangers;
the fatherless and the widow he sustains,
but the way of the wicked he thwarts.
The LORD shall reign forever;
your God, O Zion, through all generations. Alleluia.

℟.   I will sing to my God all the days of my life.

8   Isaiah 12:2-3, 4, 5-6

℟.   Praise the Lord and call upon his name.

God indeed is my savior;
   I am confident and unafraid.
My strength and my courage is the LORD,
   and he has been my savior.
With joy you will draw water
   at the fountain of salvation.

℟.   Praise the Lord and call upon his name.

Give thanks to the LORD, acclaim his name;
   among the nations make known his deeds,
   proclaim how exalted is his name.

℟.   Praise the Lord and call upon his name.

Sing praise to the LORD for his glorious achievement;
   let this be known throughout all the earth.
Shout with exultation, O city of Zion,
   for great in your midst
   is the Holy One of Israel!

℟.   Praise the Lord and call upon his name.

9   Isaiah 61:10, 11

℟.   My spirit rejoices in my God.

I rejoice heartily in the LORD,
   in my God is the joy of my soul;
For he has clothed me with a robe of salvation,
   and wrapped me in a mantle of justice,
Like a bridegroom adorned with a diadem,
   like a bride bedecked with her jewels.

℟.   My spirit rejoices in my God.

As the earth brings forth its plants,
    and a garden makes its growth spring up,
So will the Lord God make justice and praise
    spring up before all the nations.

℟.   My spirit rejoices in my God.

10   Jeremiah 31:10, 11-12a, 12b-13, 14

℟.   The Lord has redeemed his people.

Hear the word of the LORD, O nations,
    proclaim it on distant coasts, and say:
He who scattered Israel, now gathers them together,
    he guards them as a shepherd his flock.

℟.   The Lord has redeemed his people.

The LORD shall ransom Jacob,
    he shall redeem him from the hand of his conqueror.
Shouting, they shall mount the heights of Zion,
    they shall come streaming to the LORD's blessings:

℟.   The Lord has redeemed his people.

The grain, the wine, and the oil,
    the sheep and the oxen;
They themselves shall be like watered gardens,
    never again shall they languish.

℟.   The Lord has redeemed his people.

Then the virgins shall make merry and dance,
    and young men and old as well.
I will turn their mourning into joy,
    I will console and gladden them after their sorrows.

℟.   The Lord has redeemed his people.

I will lavish choice portions upon the priests,
    and my people shall be filled with my blessings,
    says the LORD.

℟. The Lord has redeemed his people.

11 Daniel 3:52, 53, 54, 55, 56, 57

℟. Bless the Lord, all the works of his hand: praise and glorify him for ever.

**"Blessed are you, O Lord, the God of our fathers,
praiseworthy and exalted above all forever;
And blessed is your holy and glorious name,
praiseworthy and exalted above all for all ages."**

℟. Bless the Lord, all the works of his hand: praise and glorify him for ever.

**"Blessed are you in the temple of your holy glory,
praiseworthy and glorious above all forever."**

℟. Bless the Lord, all the works of his hand: praise and glorify him for ever.

**"Blessed are you on the throne of your Kingdom,
praiseworthy and exalted above all forever."**

℟. Bless the Lord, all the works of his hand: praise and glorify him for ever.

**"Blessed are you who look into the depths
from your throne upon the cherubim,
praiseworthy and exalted above all forever."**

℟. Bless the Lord, all the works of his hand: praise and glorify him for ever.

**"Blessed are you in the firmament of heaven,
praiseworthy and glorious forever."**

℟. Bless the Lord, all the works of his hand: praise and glorify him for ever.

**"Bless the Lord, all you works of the Lord,
praise and exalt him above all forever."**

℟. Bless the Lord, all the works of his hand: praise and glorify him for ever.

12   Luke 1:46-47, 48-49, 50-51, 52-53, 54-55

℟. The Lord has remembered his mercy.

**"My soul proclaims the greatness of the Lord,
  my spirit rejoices in God my Savior."**

℟. The Lord has remembered his mercy.

**"For he has looked with favor on his lowly servant.
From this day all generations will call me blessed:
  the Almighty has done great things for me,
  and holy is his Name."**

℟. The Lord has remembered his mercy.

**"He has mercy on those who fear him
  in every generation.
He has shown the strength of his arm,
  and has scattered the proud in their conceit."**

℟. The Lord has remembered his mercy.

**"He has cast down the mighty from their thrones,
  and has lifted up the lowly.
He has filled the hungry with good things,
  and the rich he has sent away empty."**

℟. The Lord has remembered his mercy.

**"He has come to the help of his servant Israel
  for he has remembered his promise of mercy,
The promise he made to our fathers,
  to Abraham and his children for ever."**

℟. The Lord has remembered his mercy.

13   Ephesians 1:3-4a, 4b-6, 7-8a, 8b-10

℟.   Blessed be God who chose us in Christ.

Blessed be the God and Father of our Lord Jesus Christ,
    who has blessed us in Christ
    with every spiritual blessing in the heavens,
as he chose us in him,
    before the foundation of the world,
    to be holy and without blemish before him.

℟.   Blessed be God who chose us in Christ.

In love he destined us for adoption
    to himself through Jesus Christ,
    in accord with the favor of his will,
for the praise of the glory of his grace
    that he granted us in the beloved.

℟.   Blessed be God who chose us in Christ.

In him we have redemption by his Blood,
    the forgiveness of transgressions,
in accord with the riches of his grace
    that he lavished upon us.

℟.   Blessed be God who chose us in Christ.

In all wisdom and insight, he has made known to us
    the mystery of his will in accord with his favor
that he set forth in him as a plan for the fullness of times,
    to sum up all things in Christ,
    in heaven and on earth.

℟.   Blessed be God who chose us in Christ.

14   Revelation 15:3, 4

℟.   Great and wonderful are all your works, Lord.

They sang the song of Moses, the servant of God,
    and the song of the Lamb:

"Great and wonderful are your works,
　　Lord God almighty.
Just and true are your ways,
　　O king of the nations.

　　℟.　Great and wonderful are all your works, Lord.

Who will not fear you, Lord,
　　or glorify your name?
For you alone are holy.
　　All the nations will come
　　and worship before you,
　　for your righteous acts have been revealed."

　　℟.　Great and wonderful are all your works, Lord.

CONCLUDING PRAYERS

207.

Father, all-powerful and ever-living God,
we do well always and everywhere to give you thanks.

When you punish us, you show your justice;
when you pardon us, you show your kindness;
yet always your mercy enfolds us.

When you chastise us, you do not wish to condemn us;
when you spare us, you give us time to make amends for our
　　sins
through Christ our Lord.

　　℟.　Amen.

208.

Lord God,
creator and ruler of your kingdom of light,
in your great love for this world
you gave up your only Son

for our salvation.
His cross has redeemed us,
his death has given us life,
his resurrection has raised us to glory.
Through him we ask you
to be always present among your family.
Teach us to be reverent in the presence of your glory;
fill our hearts with faith,
our days with good works,
our lives with your love;
may your truth be on our lips
and your wisdom in all our actions,
that we may receive the reward of everlasting life.

We ask this through Christ our Lord.

 ℟. Amen.

  209.

Lord Jesus Christ,
your loving, forgiveness knows no limits.
You took our human nature
to give us an example of humility
and to make us faithful in every trial.
May we never lose the gifts you have given us,
but if we fall into sin
lift us up by your gift of repentance,
for you live and reign for ever and ever.

 ℟. Amen.

  210.

Father,
in your love you have brought us
from evil to good and from misery to happiness.
Through your blessings

give the courage of perseverance
to those you have called and justified by faith.

Grant this through Christ our Lord.

℟.   Amen.

211.

**God and Father of us all,
you have forgiven our sins
and sent us your peace.
Help us to forgive each other
and to work together to establish peace in the world.**

We ask this through Christ our Lord.

℟.   Amen.

212.

**And may the blessing of almighty God,
the Father, and the Son, ✚ and the Holy Spirit,
come upon you and remain with you for ever.**

℟.   Amen.

213.

**May the Father bless us,
for we are his children, born to eternal life.**

℟.   Amen.

**May the Son show us his saving power,
for he died and rose for us.**

℟.   Amen.

**May the Spirit give us his gift of holiness
and lead us by the right path,
for he dwells in our hearts.**

℟.   Amen.

214.

May the Father bless us,
for he has adopted us as his children.

℞.   Amen.

May the Son come to help us,
for he has received us as brothers and sisters.

℞.   Amen.

May the Spirit be with us,
for he has made us his dwelling place.

℞.   Amen.

APPENDIX I

ABSOLUTION FROM CENSURES

1. The form of absolution is not to be changed when a priest, in keeping with the provision of law, absolves a properly disposed penitent within the sacramental forum from a censure *latae sententiae*. It is enough that the confessor intend to absolve also from censures. Before absolving from sins, however, the confessor may absolve from the censure, using the formula which is given below for absolution from censure outside the sacrament of penance.

2. When a priest, in accordance with the law, absolves a penitent from a censure outside the sacrament of penance, he uses the following formula:

**By the power granted to me,
I absolve you
from the bond of excommunication
    (or suspension or interdict).
In the name of the Father, and of the Son, ✛
and of the Holy Spirit.**

The penitent answers:

Amen.

DISPENSATION FROM IRREGULARITY

3. When, in accordance with the law, a priest dispenses a penitent from an irregularity, either during confession, after absolution has been given, or outside the sacrament of penance, he says:

**By the power granted to me
I dispense you from the irregularity
which you have incurred.
In the name of the Father, and of the Son, ✛
and of the Holy Spirit.**

The penitent answers:

Amen.

APPENDIX II

SAMPLE PENITENTIAL SERVICES

These services have been prepared by the Congregation for Divine Worship to help those who prepare or lead penitential celebrations.

PREPARING PENITENTIAL CELEBRATIONS

1. Penitential celebrations, mentioned in the *Rite of Penance* (nos. 36-37), are beneficial in fostering the spirit and virtue of penance among individuals and communities; they also help in preparing for a more fruitful celebration of the sacrament of penance. However, the faithful must be reminded of the difference between these celebrations and sacramental confession and absolution.[1]

2. The particular conditions of life, the manner of speaking, and the educational level of the congregation or special group should be taken into consideration. Thus liturgical commissions[2] and individual Christian communities preparing these celebrations should choose the texts and format most suited to the circumstances of each particular group.

3. To this end, several examples of penitential celebrations are given below. These are models and should be adapted to the specific conditions and needs of each community.

4. When the sacrament of penance is celebrated in these services, it follows the readings and homily, and the rite of reconciling several penitents with individual confession and absolution is used (nos. 54-59, *Rite of Penance*); when permitted by law, the rite for general confession and absolution is used (nos. 60-63, *Rite of Penance*).

---

[1] See Congregation for the Doctrine of the Faith, *Normae pastorales circa absolutionem sacramentalem generali modo impertiendam*, June 16, 1972, no. X: *AAS* 64 (1972) 513.

[2] See Congregation of Rites, Instruction *Inter Occumenici*, September 26, 1964, no. 39: *AAS* 56 (1964) 110.

I. PENITENTIAL CELEBRATIONS DURING LENT

5. Lent is the principal time of penance both for individual Christians and for the whole Church. It is therefore desirable to prepare the Christian community for a fuller sharing in the paschal mystery by penitential celebrations during Lent.[1]

6. Texts from the lectionary and sacramentary may be used in these penitential celebrations; the penitential nature of the liturgy of the word in the Masses for Lent should be considered.

7. Two outlines of penitential celebrations suitable for Lent are given here. The first emphasizes penance as strengthening or restoring baptismal grace; the second shows penance as a preparation for a fuller sharing in the Easter mystery of Christ and his Church.

FIRST EXAMPLE

PENANCE LEADS TO A STRENGTHENING OF BAPTISMAL GRACE

8. (a) After an appropriate song and the greeting by the minister, the meaning of this celebration is explained to the people. It prepares the Christian community to recall their baptismal grace at the Easter Vigil and to reach newness of life in Christ through freedom from sins.

9. (b) PRAYER

My brothers and sisters, we have neglected the gifts of our baptism and fallen into sin. Let us ask God to renew his grace within us as we turn to him in repentance.

Let us kneel (or: Bow your heads before God).

All pray in silence for a brief period.

Let us stand (or: Raise your heads).

Lord Jesus,
you redeemed us by your passion
and raised us to new life in baptism.
Protect us with your unchanging love

---

[1] See Second Vatican Council, constitution *Sacrosanctum Concilium*, no. 109; Paul VI, Apostolic Constitution *Paenitemini*, February 17, 1966, no. IX: *AAS* 58 (1966) 185.

**and share with us the joy of your resurrection,
for you live and reign for ever and ever.**

℞. Amen.

10. (c) READINGS

FIRST READING   1 Cor 10:1-13

A reading from the first Letter of
Saint Paul to the Corinthians

I do not want you to be unaware, brothers
and sisters,
that our ancestors were all under the
cloud
and all passed through the sea,
and all of them were baptized into
Moses
in the cloud and in the sea.
All ate the same spiritual food,
and all drank the same spiritual drink,
for they drank from a spiritual rock that
followed them,
and the rock was the Christ.
Yet God was not pleased with most of
them,
for they were struck down in the desert.
These things happened as examples for us,
so that we might not desire evil things,
as they did.
And do not become idolaters, as some of
them did,
as it is written,
*The people sat down to eat and drink,
and rose up to revel.*
Let us not indulge in immorality as some
of them did,
and twenty-three thousand fell within a
single day.
Let us not test Christ as some of them did,
and suffered death by serpents.
Do not grumble as some of them did,
and suffered death by the destroyer.
These things happened to them as an example,
and they have been written down as a
warning to us,
upon whom the end of the ages has
come.
Therefore, whoever thinks he is standing
secure should take care not to fall.
No trial has come to you but what is
human.
God is faithful and will not let you be
tried beyond your strength;
but with the trial he will also provide
a way out,
so that you may be able to bear it.

The word of the Lord.

RESPONSORIAL PSALM
Ps 106:6-10, 13-14, 19-22

℞. (4) Lord, remember us, for the love you
bear your people.

We have sinned, we and our fathers;
we have committed crimes; we have
done wrong.
Our fathers in Egypt
considered not your wonders;
They remembered not your abundant
kindness,
but rebelled against the Most High at the
Red Sea.

℞. Lord, remember us, for the love you
bear your people.

Yet he saved them for his name's sake,
to make known his power.
He rebuked the Red Sea, and it was dried
up,
and he led them through the deep as
through a desert.
He saved them from hostile hands
and freed them from the hands of the
enemy.

℞. Lord, remember us, for the love you
bear your people.

But soon they forgot his works;
  they waited not for his counsel.
They gave way to craving in the desert
  and tempted God in the wilderness.

℟. Lord, remember us, for the love you
  bear your people.

They made a calf in Horeb
  and adored a molten image;
They exchanged their glory
  for the image of a grass-eating bullock.

℟. Lord, remember us, for the love you
  bear your people.

They forgot the God who had saved them,
  who had done great deeds in Egypt,
Wondrous deeds in the land of Ham,
  terrible things at the Red Sea.

℟. Lord, remember us, for the love you
  bear your people.

GOSPEL   Lk 15:4-7

✠ A reading from the holy Gospel
  according to Luke

Jesus addressed this parable to them:
"What man among you having a hundred
  sheep and losing one of them
  would not leave the ninety-nine in the
  desert
  and go after the lost one until he finds
  it?
And when he does find it,
  he sets it on his shoulders with great joy
  and, upon his arrival home,
  he calls together his friends and neighbors and says to them,
  'Rejoice with me because I have found
  my lost sheep.'
I tell you, in just the same way
  there will be more joy in heaven over
  one sinner who repents
  than over ninety-nine righteous people
  who have no need of repentance."
        The Gospel of the Lord.

---

2   Lk 15:11-32

✠ A reading from the holy Gospel
  according to Luke

Jesus addressed this parable to them:
"A man had two sons, and the younger
  son said to his father,
  'Father, give me the share of your estate
  that should come to me.'"
So the father divided the property between
  them.
After a few days, the younger son collected
  all his belongings
  and set off to a distant country
  where he squandered his inheritance on a
  life of dissipation.
When he had freely spent everything,
  a severe famine struck that country,
  and he found himself in dire need.
So he hired himself out to one of the local
  citizens
  who sent him to his farm to tend the
  swine.
And he longed to eat his fill of the pods on
  which the swine fed,
  but nobody gave him any.
Coming to his senses he thought,
  'How many of my father's hired workers
  have more than enough food to eat,
  but here am I, dying from hunger.
I shall get up and go to my father and I shall
  say to him,
  "Father, I have sinned against heaven
  and against you.
I no longer deserve to be called your son;
  treat me as you would treat one of your
  hired workers."'
So he got up and went back to his father.
While he was still a long way off,
  his father caught sight of him, and was
  filled with compassion.
He ran to his son, embraced him and kissed
  him.
His son said to him,
  'Father, I have sinned against heaven and
  against you;
  I no longer deserve to be called your son.'
But his father ordered his servants,
  'Quickly, bring the finest robe and put it
  on him;

put a ring on his finger and sandals on his
feet.
Take the fattened calf and slaughter it.
Then let us celebrate with a feast,
because this son of mine was dead, and
has come to life again;
he was lost, and has been found.'
Then the celebration began.
Now the older son had been out in the
field
and, on his way back, as he neared the
house,
he heard the sound of music and dancing.
He called one of the servants and asked
what this might mean.
The servant said to him,
'Your brother has returned
and your father has slaughtered the fattened calf
because he has him back safe and sound.'

He became angry,
and when he refused to enter the house,
his father came out and pleaded with him.
He said to his father in reply,
'Look, all these years I served you
and not once did I disobey your orders;
yet you never gave me even a young goat
to feast on with my friends.
But when your son returns
who swallowed up your property with
prostitutes,
for him you slaughter the fattened calf.'
He said to him,
'My son, you are here with me always;
everything I have is yours.
But now we must celebrate and rejoice,
because your brother was dead and has
come to life again;
he was lost and has been found.' "
The Gospel of the Lord.

11. (d) HOMILY

The celebrant may speak about:

—the need to fulfill the grace of baptism by living faithfully the Gospel
of Christ (see 1 Corinthians 10:1-13);

—the seriousness of sin committed after baptism (see Hebrews 6:4-8);

—the unlimited mercy of our God and Father who continually welcomes
those who turn back to him after having sinned (see Luke 15);

—Easter as the feast when the Church rejoices over the Christian initia-
tion of catechumens and the reconciliation of penitents.

12. (e) Examination of conscience

After the homily, the examination of conscience takes place; a sample
text is given in Appendix III, page 215. A period of silence should always be included so that each person may personally examine his conscience. In a special way the people should examine their conscience on
the baptismal promises which will be renewed at the Easter Vigil.

13. (f) ACT OF REPENTANCE

The deacon (or another minister, if there is no deacon) speaks to the assembly:

**My brothers and sisters, the hour of God's favor draws near,
the day of his mercy and of our salvation, when death was**

destroyed and eternal life began. This is the season for planting new vines in God's vineyard, the time for pruning the vines to ensure a richer harvest.

We all acknowledge that we are sinners. We are moved to penance, encouraged by the example and prayers of our brothers and sisters. We admit our guilt and say: "Lord, I acknowledge my sins; my offenses are always before me. Turn away your face, Lord, from my sins, and blot out all my wrong-doing. Give me back the joy of your salvation and give me a new and steadfast spirit."

We are sorry for having offended God by our sins. May he be merciful and hear us as we ask to be restored to his friendship and numbered among the living who share the joy of Christ's risen life.

> Then the priest sprinkles the congregation with holy water, while all sing (say):

Cleanse us, Lord, from all our sins;
wash us, and we shall be whiter than snow.

> Then the priest says:

Lord our God,
you created us in love
and redeemed us in mercy.
While we were exiled from heaven
by the jealousy of the evil one,
you gave us your only Son,
who shed his blood to save us.
Send now your Holy Spirit
to breathe new life into your children,
for you do not want us to die
but to live for you alone.
You do not abandon those who abandon you;
correct us as a Father
and restore us to your family.

Lord,
your sons and daughters stand before you
in humility and trust.
Look with compassion on us
as we confess our sins.
Heal our wounds;
stretch out a hand of pity
to save us and raise us up.
Keep us free from harm
as members of Christ's body,
as sheep of your flock,
as children of your family.
Do not allow the enemy
to triumph over us
or death to claim us for ever,
for you raised us to new life in baptism.

Hear, Lord, the prayers we offer from contrite hearts.
Have pity on us as we acknowledge our sins.
Lead us back to the way of holiness.
Protect us now and always
from the wounds of sin.
May we ever keep safe in all its fullness
the gift your love once gave us
and your mercy now restores.

We ask this through our Lord Jesus Christ, your Son,
who lives and reigns with you and the Holy Spirit,
one God, for ever and ever.
 ℟.   Amen.

> The celebration ends with an appropriate song and the dismissal of the people.

SECOND EXAMPLE

PENANCE PREPARES FOR A FULLER SHARING IN THE PASCHAL MYSTERY OF CHRIST FOR THE SALVATION OF THE WORLD

14. (a) After an appropriate song and the greeting by the minister, the faithful are briefly reminded that they are linked with each other in sin and in repentance so that each should take his calling to conversion as an occasion of grace for the whole community.

15. (b) PRAYER

My brothers and sisters, let us pray that by penance we may be united with Christ, who was crucified for our sins, and so share with all mankind in his resurrection.

Let us kneel (or: Bow your heads before God).

All pray in silence for a brief period.

Let us stand (or: Raise your heads).

1

Lord, our God and Father,
through the passion of your Son
you gave us new life.
By our practice of penance
make us one with him in his dying
so that we and all mankind
may be one with him
 in his resurrection.

We ask this through Christ our Lord.

R̹.   Amen.

2

Almighty and merciful Father,
send your Holy Spirit
to inspire and strengthen us,
so that by always carrying
the death of Jesus in our bodies
we may also show forth the power of his risen life.

We ask this through Christ our Lord.

R̹.   Amen.

16. (c) READINGS

FIRST READING　　　　Is 53:1-7, 10-12

A reading from the Book of the Prophet Isaiah

Who would believe what we have
　heard?
　To whom has the arm of the Lord been
　revealed?
He grew up like a sapling before him,
　like a shoot from the parched earth;
There was in him no stately bearing to
　make us look at him,
　nor appearance that would attract us to
　him.
He was spurned and avoided by people,
　a man of suffering, accustomed to infir-
　mity,
One of those from whom people hide their
　faces,
　spurned, and we held him in no esteem.
Yet it was our infirmities that he bore,
　our sufferings that he endured,
While we thought of him as stricken,
　as one smitten by God and afflicted.
But he was pierced for our offenses,
　crushed for our sins;
Upon him was the chastisement that
　makes us whole,
　by his stripes we were healed.
We had all gone astray like sheep,
　each following his own way;
But the Lord laid upon him
　the guilt of us all.

Though he was harshly treated, he submit-
　ted
　and opened not his mouth;
Like a lamb led to the slaughter
　or a sheep before the shearers,
　he was silent and opened not his mouth.
But the Lord was pleased
　to crush him in infirmity.
If he gives his life as an offering for sin,
　he shall see his descendants in a long
　life,
　and the will of the Lord shall be accom-
　plished through him.

Because of his affliction
　he shall see the light in fullness of days;
Through his suffering, my servant shall
　justify many,
　and their guilt he shall bear.
Therefore I will give him his portion
　among the great,
　and he shall divide the spoils with the
　mighty,
Because he surrendered himself to death
　and was counted among the wicked;
And he shall take away the sins of many,
　and win pardon for their offenses.

The word of the Lord.

RESPONSORIAL PSALM　　Ps 22:2-3, 7-9,
18-19, 20-22, 23-24, 25, 26-27, 28

R̸.　Father, your will be done.

My God, my God, why have you forsaken
　me,
　far from my prayer, from the words of
　my cry?
O my God, I cry out by day, and you an-
　swer not;
　by night, and there is no relief for me.

R̸.　Father, your will be done.

But I am a worm, not a man;
　the scorn of men, despised by the people.
All who see me scoff at me;
　they mock me with parted lips, they wag
　their heads;
"He relied on the Lord; let him deliver
　him,
　let him rescue him if he loves him."

R̸.　Father, your will be done.

I can count all my bones.
They look on and gloat over me;
　they divide my garments among them,
　and for my vesture they cast lots.

R̸.　Father, your will be done.

But you, O Lord, be not far from me;
　O my help, hasten to aid me.
Rescue my soul from the sword,
　my loneliness from the grip of the dog.
Save me from the lion's mouth;
　from the horns of the wild bulls, my
　wretched life.

℟. Father, your will be done.

I will proclaim your name to my brethren;
in the midst of the assembly I will praise
you;
"You who fear the LORD, praise him;
all you descendants of Jacob, give glory to
him;
revere him, all you descendants of Israel!"

℟. Father, your will be done.

"For he has not spurned or disdained
the wretched man in his misery,
Nor did he turn his face away from him
but when he cried out to him, he heard
him."

℟. Father, your will be done.

So by your gift I will utter praise in the vast
assembly;
I will fulfill my vows before those who
fear him.
The lowly shall eat their fill;
they who seek the LORD shall praise him;
"May your hearts be ever merry!"

℟. Father, your will be done.

All the ends of the earth
shall remember and turn to the LORD;
All the families of the nations
shall bow down before him.

℟. Father, your will be done.

SECOND READING   1 Pt 2:20b-25
A reading from the first Letter
of Saint Peter

Beloved:
If you are patient when you suffer for
doing what is good,
this is a grace before God.
For to this you have been called,
because Christ also suffered for you,
leaving you an example that you should
follow in his footsteps.
*He committed no sin, and no deceit was
found in his mouth.*
When he was insulted, he returned no insult;
when he suffered, he did not threaten;

instead, he handed himself over to the
one who judges justly.
He himself bore our sins in his body upon
the Cross,
so that, free from sin, we might live for
righteousness.
By his wounds you have been healed.
For you had gone astray like sheep,
but you have now returned to the shepherd and guardian of your souls.

The word of the Lord.

GOSPEL ACCLAMATION

Glory to you, Lord; you were given up to
death for our sins and rose again for our
justification. Glory to you, Lord.

Or an appropriate song may be sung.

GOSPEL   Mk 10:32-45

(LONG FORM)

✠ A reading from the holy Gospel
according to Mark

The disciples were on the way, going up to
Jerusalem,
and Jesus went ahead of them.
They were amazed, and those who followed were afraid.
Taking the Twelve aside again, he began
to tell them
what was going to happen to him.
"Behold, we are going up to Jerusalem,
and the Son of Man
will be handed over to the chief priests
and the scribes,
and they will condemn him to death
and hand him over to the Gentiles who
will mock him,
spit upon him, scourge him, and put him
to death,
but after three days he will rise."
Then James and John, the sons of Zebe-
dee,
came to Jesus and said to him,
"Teacher, we want you to do for us
whatever we ask of you."

He replied, "What do you wish me to do for you?"
They answered him,
  "Grant that in your glory
  we may sit one at your right and the other at your left."
Jesus said to them, "You do not know what you are asking.
Can you drink the chalice that I drink
  or be baptized with the baptism with which I am baptized?"
They said to him, "We can."
Jesus said to them, "The chalice that I drink, you will drink,
  and with the baptism with which I am baptized, you will be baptized;
  but to sit at my right or at my left is not mine to give
  but is for those for whom it has been prepared."
When the ten heard this, they became indignant at James and John.
Jesus summoned them and said to them,
  "You know that those who are recognized as rulers over the Gentiles
  lord it over them,
  and their great ones make their authority over them felt.
But it shall not be so among you.
Rather, whoever wishes to be great among you will be your servant;
  whoever wishes to be first among you will be the slave of all.
For the Son of Man did not come to be served but to serve
  and to give his life as a ransom for many."

The Gospel of the Lord.

OR

Mk 10:32-34, 42-45

(SHORT FORM)

✠ A reading from the holy Gospel according to Mark

The disciples were on the way, going up to Jerusalem,
  and Jesus went ahead of them.
They were amazed, and those who followed were afraid.
Taking the Twelve aside again, he began to tell them
  what was going to happen to him.
"Behold, we are going up to Jerusalem, and the Son of Man
  will be handed over to the chief priests and the scribes,
  and they will condemn him to death
  and hand him over to the Gentiles who will mock him,
  spit upon him, scourge him, and put him to death,
  but after three days he will rise."

Jesus summoned them and said to them,
  "You know that those who are recognized as rulers over the Gentiles
  lord it over them,
  and their great ones make their authority over them felt.
But it shall not be so among you.
Rather, whoever wishes to be great among you will be your servant;
  whoever wishes to be first among you will be the slave of all.
For the Son of Man did not come to be served but to serve
  and to give his life as a ransom for many."

The Gospel of the Lord.

17. (d) HOMILY

The celebrant may speak about:

—sin, by which we offend God and also Christ's body, the Church, whose members we became in baptism;

—sin as a failure of love for Christ who in the paschal mystery showed his love for us to the end;

—the way we affect each other when we do good or choose evil;

—the mystery of vicarious satisfaction by which Christ bore the burden of our sins, so that by his wounds we would be healed (see Isaiah 53; 1 Peter 2:24).

—the social and ecclesial dimension of penance by which individual Christians share in the work of converting the whole community;

—the celebration of Easter as the feast of the Christian community which is renewing itself by the conversion or repentance of each member, so that the Church may become a clearer sign of salvation in the world.

18. (e) EXAMINATION OF CONSCIENCE

After the homily, the examination of conscience takes place; a sample text is given in Appendix III, page **215**. A period of silence should always be included so that each person may personally examine his conscience.

19. (f) ACT OF REPENTANCE

After the examination of conscience, all say together:

**I confess to almighty God,
and to you, my brothers and sisters,
that I have sinned through my own fault**

They strike their breast:

**in my thoughts and in my words,
in what I have done,
and in what I have failed to do;
and I ask blessed Mary, ever virgin,
all the angels and saints,
and you, my brothers and sisters,
to pray for me to the Lord our God.**

As a sign of conversion and charity toward others, it should be suggested that the faithful give something to help the poor to celebrate the feast of Easter with joy; or they might visit the sick, or make up for some injustice in the community, or perform similar works.

Then the **Lord's Prayer** may be said, which the priest concludes in this way:

Deliver us, Father, from every evil as we unite ourselves through penance with the saving passion of your Son. Grant us a share in the joy of the resurrection of Jesus who is Lord for ever and ever.

℞. Amen.

Depending on circumstances, the general confession may be followed by a form of devotion such as adoration of the cross or the way of the cross, according to local customs and the wishes of the people.

At the end, an appropriate song is sung, and the people are sent away with a greeting or blessing.

II. PENITENTIAL CELEBRATIONS DURING ADVENT

20. (a) After an appropriate song and the greeting by the minister, the meaning of the celebration is explained in these or similar words:

1

My brothers and sisters, Advent is a time of preparation, when we make ready to celebrate the mystery of our Lord's coming as man, the beginning of our redemption. Advent also moves us to look forward with renewed hope to the second coming of Christ, when God's plan of salvation will be brought to fulfillment. We are reminded too of our Lord's coming to each one of us at the hour of our death. We must make sure that he will find us prepared for his coming, as the gospel tells us: "Blessed are those servants who are found awake when the Lord comes" (Luke 12:37). This service of penance is meant to make us ready in mind and heart for the coming of Christ, which we are soon to celebrate in the Mass of Christmas.

2 (Romans 13:11-12)

Now it is time for you to wake from sleep, for our salvation is nearer to us than it was when we first believed. The night is ending; the day draws near. Let us then cast off the deeds of darkness and put on the armor of light. Let us live honestly as people do in the daylight, not in carousing and drunkenness, not in lust and debauchery, not in quarreling and jealousy. But rather let us put on the Lord Jesus Christ and give no thought to the desires of the flesh.

21. (b) PRAYER

My brothers and sisters, we look forward to celebrating the mystery of Christ's coming on the feast of Christmas. Let us pray that when he comes he may find us awake and ready to receive him.

All pray in silence for a brief period.

1

Lord our God,
maker of the heavens,
as we look forward to the coming of our redeemer
grant us the forgiveness of our sins.
We ask this through Christ our Lord. ℟. Amen.

2

Eternal Son of God,
creator of the human family
and our redeemer,
come at last among us
as the child of the immaculate Virgin,
and redeem the world.
Reveal your loving presence
by which you set us free from sin
in becoming one like us
in all things but sin,
for you live and reign for ever and ever. ℟. Amen.

22. (c) READINGS

FIRST READING   Mal 3:1-7a

**A reading from the Book of the
Prophet Malachi**

Lo, I am sending my messenger
  to prepare the way before me;
And suddenly there will come to the tem-
  ple
  the Lord whom you seek,
And the messenger of the covenant whom
    you desire.
    Yes, he is coming, says the Lord of
      hosts.
But who will endure the day of his com-
  ing?
  And who can stand when he appears?
For he is like the refiner's fire,
  or like the fuller's lye.
He will sit refining and purifying silver,
  and he will purify the sons of Levi,
Refining them like gold or like silver
    that they may offer due sacrifice to the
      Lord.
Then the sacrifice of Judah and Jerusalem
    will please the Lord,
    as in days of old, as in years gone
      by.
I will draw near to you for judgment,
  and I will be swift to bear witness
Against the sorcerers, adulterers, and per-
  jurers,
    those who defraud the hired man of his
      wages,
Against those who defraud widows and or-
  phans;
    those who turn aside the stranger,
    and those who do not fear me, says the
      Lord of hosts.
Surely I, the Lord, do not change,
  nor do you cease to be sons of Jacob.
Since the days of your fathers you have
    turned aside
  from my statutes, and have not kept
    them.
Return to me, and I will return to you,
  says the Lord of hosts.

The word of the Lord.

RESPONSORIAL PSALM   Ps 85:2-3, 4-5, 6-8, 9-10, 11-12, 13-14

℟. Lord, let us see your kindness, and grant
  us your salvation.

You have favored, O Lord, your land;
  you have restored the well-being of
    Jacob.
You have forgiven the guilt of your people;
  you have covered all their sins.

℟. Lord, let us see your kindness, and grant
  us your salvation.

You have withdrawn all your wrath;
  you have revoked your burning anger.
Restore us, O God, our savior,
  and abandon your displeasure against
    us.

℟. Lord, let us see your kindness, and grant
  us your salvation.

Will you be ever angry with us,
  prolonging your anger to all genera-
    tions?
Will you not instead give us life;
  and shall not your people rejoice in you:
Show us, Lord, your mercy,
  and grant us your salvation.

℟. Lord, let us see your kindness, and grant
  us your salvation.

I will hear what God proclaims;
  the Lord—for he proclaims peace to his
    people.
Near indeed is his salvation to those who
    fear him,
  glory dwelling in our land.

℟. Lord, let us see your kindness, and grant
  us your salvation.

Kindness and truth shall meet;
  justice and peace shall kiss.
Truth shall spring out of the earth,
  and justice shall look down from heaven.

℟. Lord, let us see your kindness, and grant
  us your salvation.

The Lord himself will give his benefits;
  our land shall yield its increase.
Justice shall walk before him,
  and prepare the way of his steps.

℟. Lord, let us see your kindness, and grant us your salvation.

SECOND READING   Rv 21:1-12

A reading from the Book of Revelation

Then I saw a new heaven and a new earth.
The former heaven and the former earth
    had passed away,
    and the sea was no more.
I also saw the holy city, a new Jerusalem,
    coming down out of heaven from God,
    prepared as a bride adorned for her hus-
    band.
I heard a loud voice from the throne say-
    ing,
    "Behold, God"s dwelling is with the
    human race.
He will dwell with them and they will be
    his people
    and God himself will always be with
    them as their God.
He will wipe every tear from their eyes,
    and there shall be no more death or
    mourning, wailing or pain,
    for the old order has passed away."
The one who sat on the throne said,
    "Behold, I make all things new."
Then he said, "Write these words down,
    for they are trustworthy and true."
He said to me, "They are accomplished.
I am the Alpha and the Omega,
    the beginning and the end.
To the thirsty I will give a gift from the
    spring of life-giving water.
The victor will inherit these gifts,
    and I shall be his God,
    and he will be my son.
But as for cowards, the unfaithful, the de-
    praved, murderers,
    the unchaste, sorcerers, idol-worshipers,
    and deceivers of every sort,
    their lot is in the burning pool of fire and
    sulfur, which is the second death."
One of the seven angels who held the seven
    bowls
    filled with the seven last plagues
    came and said to me,

"Come here. I will show you the bride, the
    wife of the Lamb."
He took me in spirit to a great, high moun-
    tain
    and showed me the holy city Jerusalem
    coming down out of heaven from God.
It gleamed with the splendor of God.
Its radiance was like that of a precious stone,
    like jasper, clear as crystal.
It had a massive, high wall, with twelve
    gates
    where twelve angels were stationed
    and on which names were inscribed,
    the names of the twelve tribes of the chil-
    dren of Israel.

The word of the Lord.

GOSPEL ACCLAMATION

1

I am coming quickly, says the Lord, and I
will repay each man.
Come, Lord Jesus.

2

The Spirit and the Bride say: "Come."
Let all who hear answer: "Come."
Come, Lord Jesus.

Or an appropriate song may be sung.

GOSPEL

1   Mt 3:1-12

✝ A reading from the holy Gospel
    according to Matthew

John the Baptist appeared, preaching in
    the desert of Judea
    and saying, "Repent, for the Kingdom of
    heaven is at hand!"
It was of him that the prophet Isaiah had
    spoken when he said:
    A voice of one crying out in the desert,
    "Prepare the way of the Lord,
        make straight his paths."
John wore clothing made of camel's hair
    and had a leather belt around his waist.

His food was locusts and wild honey.

At that time Jerusalem, all Judea,
  and the whole region around the Jordan
  were going out to him
  and were being baptized by him in the
  Jordan River
  as they acknowledged their sins.

When he saw many of the Pharisees and
  Sadducees
  coming to his baptism, he said to them,
  "You brood of vipers!

Who warned you to flee from the coming
  wrath?

Produce good fruit as evidence of your repentance.

And do not presume to say to yourselves,
  'We have Abraham as our father.'

For I tell you,
  God can raise up children to Abraham
  from these stones.

Even now the ax lies at the root of the
  trees.

Therefore every tree that does not bear
  good fruit
  will be cut down and thrown into the
  fire.

I am baptizing you with water, for repentance,
  but the one who is coming after me is
  mightier than I.

I am not worthy to carry his sandals.

He will baptize you with the Holy Spirit
  and fire.

His winnowing fan is in his hand.

He will clear his threshing floor
  and gather his wheat into his barn,
  but the chaff he will burn with unquenchable fire."

The Gospel of the Lord.

2   Lk 3:1-17

✠ A reading from the holy Gospel
according to Luke

In the fifteenth year of the reign of
  Tiberius Caesar,
  when Pontius Pilate was governor of
  Judea,
  and Herod was tetrarch of Galilee,
  and his brother Philip tetrarch of the region of Ituraea and Trachonitis,
  and Lysanias was tetrarch of Abilene,
  during the high priesthood of Annas and
  Caiaphas,
  the word of God came to John the son of
  Zechariah in the desert.

John went throughout the whole region of
  the Jordan,
  proclaiming a baptism of repentance for
  the forgiveness of sins,
  as it is written in the book of the words
  of the prophet Isaiah:
    A voice of one crying out in the desert:
    "Prepare the way of the Lord,
      make straight his paths.
    Every valley shall be filled
      and every mountain and hill shall
      be made low.
    The winding roads shall be made
      straight,
      and the rough ways made smooth,
    and all flesh shall see the salvation
      of God."

The crowds asked John the Baptist,
  "What should we do?"

He said to them in reply,
  "Whoever has two cloaks
  should share with the person who has
  none.

And whoever has food should do likewise."

Even tax collectors came to be baptized
  and they said to him,
  "Teacher, what should we do?"

He answered them,
  "Stop collecting more than what is prescribed."

Soldiers also asked him,
  "And what is it that we should do?"

He told them,
  "Do not practice extortion,

do not falsely accuse anyone,
and be satisfied with your wages."
Now the people were filled with expectation,
and all were asking in their hearts
whether John might be the Christ.
John answered them all, saying,
"I am baptizing you with water,
but one mightier than I is coming.

I am not worthy to loosen the thongs of his sandals.
He will baptize you with the Holy Spirit and fire.
His winnowing fan is in his hand to clear his threshing floor
and to gather the wheat into his barn,
but the chaff he will burn with unquenchable fire."

The Gospel of the Lord.

23. (d) EXAMINATION OF CONSCIENCE

After the homily, the examination of conscience takes place; a sample text is given in Appendix III, page **215**. A period of silence should always be included so that each person may personally examine his conscience.

24. (e) ACT OF REPENTANCE

The act of repentance follows the examination of conscience. All may say the **I confess to almighty God** or the intercessions as in no. 60.

The **Lord's Prayer** is said or sung, and is concluded by the presiding minister in this way:

1

Lord our God,
on the first day of creation
you made the light
that scatters all darkness.
Let Christ, the light of lights,
hidden from all eternity,
shine at last on your people
and free us from the darkness of sin.
Fill our lives with good works
as we go out to meet your Son,
so that we may give him a fitting welcome.
We ask this through Christ our Lord.

℟.   Amen.

2

Almighty and eternal God,
you sent your only-begotten Son
to reconcile the world to yourself.
Lift from our hearts
the oppressive gloom of sin,
so that we may celebrate
the approaching dawn of Christ's birth
with fitting joy.
We ask this through Christ our Lord.

℟. Amen.

> At the end, a song is sung, and the people are sent away with a greeting or blessing.

III. COMMON PENITENTIAL CELEBRATIONS

I. SIN AND CONVERSION

> 25. (a) After an appropriate song (for example Psalm 139:1-12, 16, 23-24) and greeting, the minister who presides briefly explains the meaning of the readings. Then he invites all to pray. After a period of silence, he concludes the prayer in this way:

Lord Jesus,
you turned and looked on Peter
when he denied you for the third time.
He wept for his sin
and turned again to you in sincere repentance.
Look now on us and touch our hearts,
so that we also may turn back to you
and be always faithful in serving you,
for you live and reign for ever and ever.

℟. Amen.

26. (b) READINGS

FIRST READING   Lk 22:31-34

✠ A reading from the holy Gospel
according to Luke

"I tell you, Peter, before the cock crows this day,
you will deny three times that you know me."

Jesus said,
"Simon, Simon, behold Satan has de-
manded
to sift all of you like wheat,
but I have prayed that your own faith
may not fail;
and once you have turned back,
you must strengthen your brothers."

He said to him,
"Lord, I am prepared to go to prison and
to die with you."
But he replied,
"I tell you, Peter, before the cock crows
this day,
you will deny three times that you know
me."

> The Gospel of the Lord.

A short period of silence follows the
reading.

SECOND READING   Lk 22:54-62

✠ A reading from the holy Gospel
according to Luke

Peter went out and began to weep bitterly.

After arresting Jesus they led him away
and took him into the house of the high
priest;
Peter was following at a distance.
They lit a fire in the middle of the courtyard
and sat around it,
and Peter sat down with them.
When a maid saw him seated in the light,
she looked intently at him and said,
"This man too was with him."
But he denied it saying,
"Woman, I do not know him."
A short while later someone else saw him
and said,
"You too are one of them";
but Peter answered, "My friend, I am
not."
About an hour later, still another insisted,
"Assuredly, this man too was with him,
for he also is a Galilean."
But Peter said,
"My friend, I do not know what you are
talking about."
Just as he was saying this, the cock crowed,
and the Lord turned and looked at Peter;
and Peter remembered the word of the
Lord,
how he had said to him,
"Before the cock crows today, you will
deny me three times."
He went out and began to weep bitterly.

> The Gospel of the Lord.

RESPONSORIAL PSALM

                Ps 31:10, 15-17, 20

℟.   My trust is in you, O God.

Have pity on me, O LORD, for I am in distress;
with sorrow my eye is consumed; my
soul also, and my body.

℟.   My trust is in you, O God.

But my trust is in you, O LORD;
I say, "You are my God."
In your hands is my destiny; rescue me
from the clutches of my enemies and my
persecutors.
Let your face shine upon your servant;
save me in your mercy.

℟.   My trust is in you, O God.

How great is the goodness, O LORD,
which you have in store for those who
fear you,
And which, toward those who take refuge
in you,
you show in the sight of men.

℟.   My trust is in you, O God.

2   Ps 51:3-4, 5-6ab, 7-8, 9-11,
12-13, 14 and 17, 19

℟.   (see 14a) Give me back the joy of your
salvation.

Have mercy on me, O God, in your goodness;
in the greatness of your compassion
wipe out my offense.
Thoroughly wash me from my guilt
and of my sin cleanse me.

℟.   Give me back the joy of your salvation.

For I acknowledge my offense,
and my sin is before me always:
"Against you only have I sinned,
and done what is evil in your sight."

℟.   Give me back the joy of your salvation.

Indeed, in guilt was I born,
and in sin my mother conceived me;

Behold, you are pleased with sincerity of heart,
and in my inmost being you teach me wisdom.

℟. Give me back the joy of your salvation.

Cleanse me of sin with hyssop, that I may be purified;
wash me, and I shall be whiter than snow.
Let me hear the sounds of joy and gladness;
the bones you have crushed shall rejoice.
Turn away your face from my sins,
and blot out all my guilt.

℟. Give me back the joy of your salvation.

A clean heart create for me, O God,
and a steadfast spirit renew within me.
Cast me not out from your presence,
and your Holy Spirit take not from me.

℟. Give me back the joy of your salvation.

Give me back the joy of your salvation,
and a willing spirit sustain in me.
O Lord, open my lips,
and my mouth shall proclaim your praise.

℟. Give me back the joy of your salvation.

My sacrifice, O God, is a contrite spirit;
a heart contrite and humbled, O God, you will not spurn.

℟. Give me back the joy of your salvation.

GOSPEL   Jn 21:15-19

✠ A reading from the holy Gospel according to John

Feed my lambs, feed my sheep.

After Jesus had revealed himself to his disciples and eaten breakfast with them,
he said to Simon Peter,
"Simon, son of John, do you love me more than these?"
Simon Peter answered him, "Yes, Lord, you know that I love you."
Jesus said to him, "Feed my lambs."
He then said to Simon Peter a second time,
"Simon, son of John, do you love me?"
Simon Peter answered him, "Yes, Lord, you know that I love you."
He said to him, "Tend my sheep."
He said to him the third time,
"Simon, son of John, do you love me?"
Peter was distressed that he had said to him a third time,
"Do you love me?" and he said to him,
"Lord, you know everything; you know that I love you."
Jesus said to him, "Feed my sheep.
Amen, amen, I say to you, when you were younger,
you used to dress yourself and go where you wanted;
but when you grow old, you will stretch out your hands,
and someone else will dress you
and lead you where you do not want to go."
He said this signifying by what kind of death he would glorify God.
And when he had said this, he said to him, "Follow me."

The Gospel of the Lord.

27. (c) HOMILY

The celebrant may speak about:

—the trust we must put in God's grace, not in our own powers;

—the faithfulness by which we as baptized Christians must live as true and faithful followers of the Lord;

—our weakness by which we often fall into sin and refuse to give witness to the gospel;

—the mercy of the Lord, who welcomes as a friend the one who turns to him with his whole heart.

28. (d) EXAMINATION OF CONSCIENCE

After the homily, the examination of conscience takes place; a sample text is given in Appendix III, page 215. A period of silence should always be included so that each person may personally examine his conscience.

29. (e) ACT OF REPENTANCE

After the examination of conscience, the presiding minister invites all to prayer in these or similar words:

God gives us an example of love: when we were sinners he first loved us and took pity on us. Let us turn to him with a sincere heart, and in the words of Peter say to him:

℞. Lord, you know all things; you know that I love you.

> A short period of silence should follow each invocation. Each invocation may be said by different individuals, the rest answering.

—Lord, like Peter we have relied on our own strength rather than on grace. Look on us, Lord, and have mercy.

℞. Lord, you know all things; you know that I love you.

—Our pride and foolishness have led us into temptation. Look on us, Lord, and have mercy.

℞. Lord, you know all things; you know that I love you.

—We have been vain and self-important. Look on us, Lord, and have mercy.

℞. Lord, you know all things; you know that I love you.

—We have at times been pleased rather than saddened by the misfortunes of others. Look on us, Lord, and have mercy.

℞. Lord, you know all things; you know that I love you.

—We have shown indifference for those in need instead of helping them. Look on us, Lord, and have mercy.

℞. Lord, you know all things; you know that I love you.

—We have been afraid to stand up for justice and truth. Look on us, Lord, and have mercy.

℞. Lord, you know all things; you know that I love you.

—We have repeatedly broken the promises of our baptism and failed to be your disciples. Look on us, Lord, and have mercy.

℞. Lord, you know all things; you know that I love you.

—Let us now pray to the Father in the words Christ gave us and ask forgiveness for our sins:

Our Father . . .

> 30. (f) After an appropriate song, the presiding minister says the final prayer and dismisses the people:

Lord Jesus, our Savior,
you called Peter to be an apostle;
when he repented of his sin
you restored him to your friendship
and confirmed him as first of the apostles.
Turn to us with love
and help us to imitate Peter's example.
Give us strength to turn from our sins
and to serve you in the future
with greater love and devotion,
for you live and reign for ever and ever.

℞.   Amen.

II. The Son Returns to the Father

> 31. (a) After an appropriate song and the greeting by the minister, the theme of the celebration is explained to the community. Then he invites all to pray. After a period of silence, he says:

Almighty God,
you are the Father of us all.
You created the human family
to dwell for ever with you

and to praise your glory.
Open our ears to hear your voice
so that we may return to you
with sincere repentance for our sins.
Teach us to see in you our loving Father,
full of compassion for all who call to you for help.
We know that you punish us only to set us free from evil
and that you are ready to forgive us our sins.
Restore your gift of salvation
which alone brings true happiness,
so that we may all return to our Father's house
and share your table
now and for ever.

℟. Amen.

32. (b) READINGS

FIRST READING   Eph 1:3-7

**A reading from the Letter of Saint Paul
to the Ephesians**

He destined us for adoption to himself.

Blessed be the God and Father of our Lord
    Jesus Christ,
   who has blessed us in Christ
   with every spiritual blessing in the heavens,
     as he chose us in him, before the foundation of the world,
     to be holy and without blemish before
     him.
In love he destined us for adoption to himself through Jesus Christ,
   in accord with the favor of his will,
   for the praise of the glory of his grace
   that he granted us in the beloved.

     The word of the Lord.

RESPONSORIAL PSALM
           Ps 27:1, 4, 7-10, 13-14

℟. The Lord is my light and my salvation.

The LORD is my light and my salvation;
   whom should I fear?
The LORD is my life's refuge;
   of whom should I be afraid?

℟. The Lord is my light and my salvation.

One thing I ask of the LORD;
   this I seek:
To dwell in the house of the LORD
   all the days of my life,
That I may gaze on the loveliness of the
   LORD
   and contemplate his temple.

℟. The Lord is my light and my salvation.

Hear, O LORD, the sound of my call;
   have pity on me, and answer me.
Of you my heart speaks; you my glance
   seeks;
   your presence, O LORD, I seek.

℟. The Lord is my light and my salvation.

Hide not your face from me;
   do not in anger repel your servant.
You are my helper; cast me not off;
   forsake me not, O God my savior.
Though my father and mother forsake me,
   yet will the LORD receive me.

℟. The Lord is my light and my salvation.

I believe that I shall see the bounty of the
   LORD
   in the land of the living.

Wait for the LORD with courage
be stouthearted, and wait for the LORD.

R̸. The Lord is my light and my salvation.

GOSPEL   Lk 15:11-32

✠ A reading from the holy Gospel
according to Luke

His father caught sight of him,
and was filled with compassion.

Jesus addressed this parable to them:
"A man had two sons, and the younger son
said to his father,
'Father, give me the share of your estate
that should come to me."
So the father divided the property between
them.
After a few days, the younger son collected
all his belongings
and set off to a distant country
where he squandered his inheritance on a
life of dissipation.
When he had freely spent everything,
a severe famine struck that country,
and he found himself in dire need.
So he hired himself out to one of the local
citizens
who sent him to his farm to tend the
swine.
And he longed to eat his fill of the pods on
which the swine fed,
but nobody gave him any.
Coming to his senses he thought,
'How many of my father's hired workers
have more than enough food to eat,
but here am I, dying from hunger.
I shall get up and go to my father and I shall
say to him,
"Father, I have sinned against heaven and
against you.
I no longer deserve to be called your son;
treat me as you would treat one of your
hired workers." '
So he got up and went back to his father.
While he was still a long way off,
his father caught sight of him, and was
filled with compassion.

He ran to his son, embraced him and kissed
him.
His son said to him,
'Father, I have sinned against heaven and
against you;
I no longer deserve to be called your son.'
But his father ordered his servants,
'Quickly, bring the finest robe and put it
on him;
put a ring on his finger and sandals on his
feet.
Take the fattened calf and slaughter it.
Then let us celebrate with a feast,
because this son of mine was dead, and
has come to life again;
he was lost, and has been found.'
Then the celebration began.
Now the older son had been out in the field
and, on his way back, as he neared the
house,
he heard the sound of music and dancing.
He called one of the servants and asked
what this might mean.
The servant said to him,
'Your brother has returned
and your father has slaughtered the fattened calf
because he has him back safe and sound.'
He became angry,
and when he refused to enter the house,
his father came out and pleaded with him.
He said to his father in reply,
'Look, all these years I served you
and not once did I disobey your orders;
yet you never gave me even a young goat
to feast on with my friends.
But when your son returns
who swallowed up your property with
prostitutes,
for him you slaughter the fattened calf.'
He said to him,
'My son, you are here with me always;
everything I have is yours.
But now we must celebrate and rejoice,
because your brother was dead and has
come to life again;
he was lost and has been found.' "
The Gospel of the Lord.

33. (c) HOMILY

The minister may speak about:

—sin as a turning away from the love that we should have for God our Father;

—the limitless mercy of our Father for his children who have sinned;

—the nature of true conversion;

—the forgiveness we extend to our brothers;

—the eucharistic banquet as the culmination of our reconciliation with the Church and with God.

34. (d) EXAMINATION OF CONSCIENCE

After the homily, the examination of conscience takes place; a sample text is given in Appendix III, page **215**. A period of silence should always be included so that each person may personally examine his conscience.

35. (e) ACT OF REPENTANCE

After the examination of conscience, the presiding minister invites all to pray:

Our God is a God of mercy, slow to anger and full of patience. He is the father who welcomes his son when he returns from a distant country. Let us pray to him with trust in his goodness:

℞. We are not worthy to be called your children.

—By our misuse of your gifts we have sinned against you.

℞. We are not worthy to be called your children.

—By straying from you in mind and heart we have sinned against you.

℞. We are not worthy to be called your children.

—By forgetting your love we have sinned against you.

℞. We are not worthy to be called your children.

—By indulging ourselves, while neglecting our true good and the good of our neighbor, we have sinned against you.

℞. We are not worthy to be called your children.

—**By failing to help our neighbor in his need we have sinned against you.**

℟. We are not worthy to be called your children.

—**By being slow to forgive we have sinned against you.**

℟. We are not worthy to be called your children.

—**By failing to remember your repeated forgiveness we have sinned against you.**

℟. We are not worthy to be called your children.

> Members of the congregation may add other invocations. A brief period of silence should follow each invocation. It may be desirable to have different individuals say each invocation.

—**Let us now call upon our Father in the words that Jesus gave us, and ask him to forgive us our sins:**

Our Father . . .

> **36.** (f) After an appropriate song, the presiding minister says the final prayer and dismisses the people:

God our Father,
you chose us to be your children,
to be holy in your sight
and happy in your presence.
Receive us as a loving Father
so that we may share the joy and love
of your holy Church.
We ask this through Christ our Lord.

℟.   Amen.

III. The Beatitudes

> **37.** (a) After an appropriate song and greeting of the minister, the person presiding explains briefly the meaning of the readings. Then he invites all to pray. After a period of silence, he says:

Lord,
open our ears and our hearts today

to the message of your Son,
so that through the power of his death and resurrection
we may walk in newness of life.
We ask this through Christ our Lord.

℟.   Amen.

38.   (b) READINGS

FIRST READING   1 Jn 1:5-9

A reading from the first Letter of Saint John

If we say, "We are without sin," we deceive ourselves.

Beloved:
This is the message that we have heard
   from Jesus Christ
   and proclaim to you: God is light,
   and in him there is no darkness at all.
If we say, "We have fellowship with him,"
   while we continue to walk in darkness,
   we lie and do not act in truth.
But if we walk in the light as he is in the
   light,
   then we have fellowship with one another,
   and the Blood of his Son Jesus cleanses
   us from all sin.
If we say, "We are without sin," we deceive ourselves,
   and the truth is not in us.
If we acknowledge our sins, he is faithful
   and just
   and will forgive our sins and cleanse us
   from every wrongdoing.

> The word of the Lord.

RESPONSORIAL PSALM
                Ps 146:5-6b, 6c-7a, 7b-8, 9-10

℟.   Lord, come and save us.

Blessed he whose help is the God of Jacob,
   whose hope is in the LORD, his God.
Who made heaven and earth,
   the sea and all that is in them.

℟.   Lord, come and save us.

The LORD keeps faith forever,
   secures justice for the oppressed,
   gives food to the hungry.

℟.   Lord, come and save us.

The LORD sets captives free;
   the LORD gives sight to the blind.
The LORD raises up those that were bowed
   down;
   the LORD loves the just.

℟.   Lord, come and save us.

The LORD protects strangers;
   the fatherless and the widow he sustains,
   but the way of the wicked he thwarts.
The LORD shall reign forever;
   your God, O Zion, through all generations. Alleluia.

℟.   Lord, come and save us.

GOSPEL   Mt 5:1-10

✠ A reading from the holy Gospel according to Matthew

Blessed are the poor in spirit,
for theirs is the Kingdom of heaven.

When Jesus saw the crowds, he went up
   the mountain,
   and after he had sat down, his disciples
   came to him.
He began to teach them, saying:

"Blessed are the poor in spirit,
   for theirs is the Kingdom of heaven.
Blessed are they who mourn,
   for they will be comforted.
Blessed are the meek,
   for they will inherit the land.

Blessed are they who hunger and thirst
   for righteousness,
  for they will be satisfied.
Blessed are the merciful,
  for they will be shown mercy.
Blessed are the clean of heart,
  for they will see God.

Blessed are the peacemakers,
   for they will be called children of God.
Blessed are they who are persecuted for
   the sake of righteousness,
  for theirs is the Kingdom of heaven."

The Gospel of the Lord.

39. (c) HOMILY

The minister may speak about:

—sin, by which we ignore the commands of Christ and act contrary to the teaching of the beatitudes;

—the firmness of our faith in the words of Jesus;

—our faithfulness in imitating Christ in our private lives, in the Christian community, and in human society;

—each beatitude.

40. (d) EXAMINATION OF CONSCIENCE

After the homily, the examination of conscience takes place; a sample text is given in Appendix III, page **215**. A period of silence should always be included so that each person may personally examine his conscience.

41. (e) ACT OF REPENTANCE

After the examination of conscience, the presiding minister invites all to pray in these or similar words:

My brothers and sisters, Jesus Christ has left an example for us to follow. Humbly and confidently let us ask him to renew us in spirit so that we may shape our lives according to the teaching of his Gospel.

—Lord Jesus Christ, you said:
"Blessed are the poor in spirit,
for theirs is the kingdom of heaven."
Yet we are preoccupied with money and worldly goods
and even try to increase them at the expense of justice.
Lamb of God, you take away the sin of the world:

℟. Have mercy on us.

—Lord Jesus Christ, you said:
"Blessed are the gentle,
for they shall inherit the earth."
Yet we are ruthless with each other,
and our world is full of discord and violence.
Lamb of God, you take away the sin of the world:

℞. Have mercy on us.

—Lord Jesus Christ, you said:
"Blessed are those who mourn,
for they shall be comforted."
Yet we are impatient under our own burdens
and unconcerned about the burdens of others.
Lamb of God, you take away the sin of the world:

℞. Have mercy on us.

—Lord Jesus Christ, you said:
"Blessed are those who hunger and thirst for justice,
for they shall be filled."
Yet we do not thirst for you, the fountain of all holiness,
and are slow to spread your influence
in our private lives or in society.
Lamb of God, you take away the sin of the world:

℞. Have mercy on us.

—Lord Jesus Christ, you said:
"Blessed are the merciful,
for they shall receive mercy."
Yet we are slow to forgive
and quick to condemn.
Lamb of God, you take away the sin of the world:

℞. Have mercy on us.

—Lord Jesus Christ, you said:
"Blessed are the clean of heart,
for they shall see God."

Yet we are prisoners of our senses and evil desires
and dare not raise our eyes to you.
Lamb of God, you take away the sin of the world:

    ℟. Have mercy on us.

—Lord Jesus Christ, you said:
"Blessed are the peacemakers,
for they shall be called children of God."
Yet we fail to make peace in our families,
in our country, and in the world.
Lamb of God, you take away the sin of the world:

    ℟. Have mercy on us.

—Lord Jesus Christ, you said:
"Blessed are those who are persecuted
for the sake of justice,
for the kingdom of heaven is theirs."
Yet we prefer to practice injustice
rather than suffer for the sake of right;
we discriminate against our neighbors
and oppress and persecute them.
Lamb of God, you take away the sin of the world:

    ℟. Have mercy on us.

—Now let us turn to God our Father and ask him to free us
from evil and prepare us for the coming of his kingdom:

    Our Father . . .

    42. (f) After an appropriate song, the presiding minister says the final prayer and dismisses the people:

Lord Jesus Christ,
gentle and humble of heart,
full of compassion and maker of peace,
you lived in poverty
and were persecuted in the cause of justice.

You chose the cross as the path to glory
to show us the way to salvation.
May we receive with joyful hearts
the word of your Gospel
and live by your example
as heirs and citizens of your kingdom,
where you live and reign for ever and ever.

R̲. Amen.

IV. FOR CHILDREN

43. This service is suitable for younger children, including those who have not yet participated in the sacrament of penance.

Theme: **GOD COMES TO LOOK FOR US**

44. The penitential celebration should be prepared with the children so that they will understand its meaning and purpose, be familiar with the songs, have at least an elementary knowledge of the biblical text to be read, and know what they are to say and in what order.

45. (a) GREETING

When the children have come together in the church or some other suitable place, the celebrant greets them in a friendly manner. Briefly he reminds them why they have come together and recounts the theme of the service. After the greeting, an opening song may be sung.

46. (b) READING

The celebrant may give a short introduction to the reading in these or similar words:

My dear children, each one of us has been baptized, and so we are all sons and daughters of God. God loves us as a Father, and he asks us to love him with all our hearts. He also wants us to be good to each other, so that we may all live happily together.

But people do not always do what God wants. They say: "I will not obey! I am going to do as I please." They disobey

God and do not want to listen to him. We, too, often act like that.

That is what we call sin. When we sin we turn our backs on God. If we do something really bad we cut ourselves off from God; we are complete strangers to him.

What does God do when someone turns away from him? What does he do when we leave the path of goodness that he has shown us, when we run the risk of losing the life of grace he has given us? Does God turn away from us when we turn away from him by our sins?

Here is what God does, in the words of Jesus himself:

47. Only one text of Scripture should be read.

GOSPEL   Lk 15:1-10

✠ A reading from the holy Gospel according to Luke

Tax collectors and sinners were all drawing near to listen to Jesus,
but the Pharisees and scribes began to complain, saying,
"This man welcomes sinners and eats with them."
So to them he addressed this parable.
"What man among you having a hundred sheep and losing one of them
would not leave the ninety-nine in the desert
and go after the lost one until he finds it?
And when he does find it,
he sets it on his shoulders with great joy
and, upon his arrival home,
he calls together his friends and neighbors and says to them,
'Rejoice with me because I have found my lost sheep.'
I tell you, in just the same way
there will be more joy in heaven over one sinner who repents
than over ninety-nine righteous people who have no need of repentance."

The Gospel of the Lord.

48. (c) HOMILY

The homily should be short, proclaiming God's love for us and preparing the ground for the examination of conscience.

49. (d) EXAMINATION OF CONSCIENCE

The celebrant should adapt the examination to the children's level of understanding by brief comments. There should be a suitable period of silence (see Appendix III, page 215).

50. (e) ACT OF REPENTANCE

This litany may be said by the celebrant or by one or more of the children, alternating with all present. Before the response, which may be sung, all should observe a brief pause.

God our Father,

—Sometimes we have not behaved as your children should.

    ℟. But you love us and come to us.

—We have given trouble to our parents and teachers.

    ℟. But you love us and come to us.

—We have quarreled and called each other names.

    ℟. But you love us and come to us.

—We have been lazy at home and in school, and have not been helpful to our parents (brothers, sisters, friends).

    ℟. But you love us and come to us.

—We have thought too much of ourselves and have told lies.

    ℟. But you love us and come to us.

—We have not done good to others when we had the chance.

    ℟. But you love us and come to us.

Now with Jesus, our brother, we come before our Father in heaven and ask him to forgive our sins:

Our Father . . .

> **51.** (f) ACT OF CONTRITION AND PURPOSE OF AMENDMENT
>
> Sorrow may be shown by some sign, for example, individual children may come to the altar or another suitable place with a candle, and light it there; if necessary, a server may help. Each child says in his own words:

Father,
I am sorry for all my sins:
for what I have done
and for what I have failed to do.
I will sincerely try to do better

especially . . . (he mentions his particular resolution).
Help me to walk by your light.

> In place of the candle, or in addition to it, the children may prepare a written prayer or resolution and place it on the altar or on a table designated for this purpose.
>
> If the number of children or other circumstances do not allow for this, the celebrant asks the children present to say the above prayer together, along with a general resolution.
>
> **52.** (g) PRAYER OF THE CELEBRANT

God our Father always seeks us out
when we walk away from the path of goodness.
He is always ready to forgive
when we have sinned.
May almighty God have mercy on us,
forgive us our sins,
and bring us to everlasting life.

℟.　Amen.

> **53.** The minister invites the children to express their thanks to God. They may do this by an appropriate hymn.
>
> Then he dismisses them.

V. FOR YOUNG PEOPLE

> **54.** The penitential celebration should be prepared with the young people so that with the celebrant, they may choose or compose the texts and songs. The readers, cantors or choir should be chosen from among them.

Theme: **RENEWAL OF OUR LIVES ACCORDING TO THE CHRISTIAN VOCATION**

> **55.** (a) GREETING
>
> This may be given in these or similar words:

Dear friends, we have come here to do penance and to make a fresh start as Christians. Many people see in penance only its difficult side, and its emphasis on sorrow.

But it has also a more joyful side, and it looks more to the future than to the past.

Through penance God calls us to a new beginning. He helps us to find our true freedom as his sons and daughters. When Jesus invites us to repentance, he is inviting us to take our place in his Father's kingdom. This is what he teaches us in the parable about the merchant who came across a pearl of great value and sold everything he had in order to buy it.

If we follow our Lord's advice we exchange our past life for one far more valuable.

> Then a song is sung; it should stress the call to a new life or following God's call with an eager heart (for example, Psalm 40:1-9 ℟. Here am I, Lord; I come to do your will).

56. (b) PRAYER

Lord our God,
you call us out of darkness into light,
out of self-deception into truth,
out of death into life.
Send us your Holy Spirit
to open our ears to your call.
Fill our hearts with courage
to be true followers of your Son.
We ask this through Christ our Lord.

℟. Amen.

57. (c) READINGS

FIRST READING Rom 7:18-25a

A reading from the Letter of Saint Paul
to the Romans

Brothers and sisters:
I know that good does not dwell in me,
  that is, in my flesh.
The willing is ready at hand, but doing the
  good is not.
For I do not do the good I want,
  but I do the evil I do not want.
Now if I do what I do not want, it is no
  longer I who do it,
  but sin that dwells in me.
So, then, I discover the principle
  that when I want to do right, evil is at
  hand.
For I take delight in the law of God, in my
  inner self,

but I see in my members another principle
at war with the law of my mind,
taking me captive to the law of sin that dwells in my members.
Miserable one that I am!
Who will deliver me from this mortal body?
Thanks be to God through Jesus Christ our Lord.

The word of the Lord.

2　Rom 8:18-25

A reading from the Letter of Saint Paul to the Romans

Brothers and sisters:
I consider that the sufferings of this present time are as nothing
compared with the glory to be revealed for us.
For creation awaits with eager expectation the revelation of the children of God;
for creation was made subject to futility,
not of its own accord but because of the one who subjected it,
in hope that creation itself
would be set free from slavery to corruption
and share in the glorious freedom of the children of God.
We know that all creation is groaning in labor pains even until now;

and not only that, but we ourselves,
who have the firstfruits of the Spirit,
we also groan within ourselves
as we wait for adoption, the redemption of our bodies.
For in hope we were saved.
Now hope that sees for itself is not hope.
For who hopes for what one sees?
But if we hope for what we do not see, we wait with endurance.

The word of the Lord.

A song is sung, or a brief period of silence is observed.

GOSPEL　Mt 13:44-46

✝ **A reading from the holy Gospel according to Matthew**

Jesus said to his disciples:
"The Kingdom of heaven is like a treasure buried in a field,
which a person finds and hides again,
and out of joy goes and sells all that he has and buys that field.
Again, the Kingdom of heaven is like a merchant
searching for fine pearls.
When he finds a pearl of great price,
he goes and sells all that he has and buys it."

The Gospel of the Lord.

58. (d) HOMILY

The celebrant may speak about:

—the law of sin which in us struggles against God;

—the necessity of giving up the way of sin so that we may enter the kingdom of God.

59. (e) EXAMINATION OF CONSCIENCE

After the homily, the examination of conscience takes place; a sample text is given in Appendix III, page **215**. A period of silence should always be included so that each person may personally examine his conscience.

60. (f) ACT OF REPENTANCE

Christ our Lord came to call sinners into his Father's kingdom. Let us now make an act of sorrow in our hearts and resolve to avoid sin in the future.

After a brief period of silence, all say together:

I confess to almighty God,
and to you, my brothers and sisters,
that I have sinned through my own fault.

They strike their breast:

in my thoughts and in my words,
in what I have done,
and in what I have failed to do;
and I ask blessed Mary, ever virgin,
all the angels and saints,
and you, my brothers and sisters,
to pray for me to the Lord our God.

Minister:

**Lord our God,
you know all things.
You know that we want to be more generous
in serving you and our neighbor.**

Look on us with love and hear our prayer.

Reader:

Give us the strength to turn away from sin.

℟. Hear our prayer.

Help us to be sorry for our sins and to keep our resolutions.

℟. Hear our prayer.

Forgive our sins and have pity on our weakness.

℟. Hear our prayer.

Give us trust in your goodness and make us generous in serving you.

℟. Hear our prayer.

Help us to be true followers of your Son and living members of his Church.

> Minister:

God does not want the sinner to die, but to turn to him and live. May he be pleased that we have confessed our sinfulness, and may he show us his great mercy as we pray in obedience to his Son.

> All say together:

Our Father . . .

> **61.** The celebration ends with an appropriate song and the dismissal.

VI. FOR THE SICK

> **62.** According to the condition of the sick people and the suitability of the place, the minister goes to the sick, gathered in one room, or else he brings them together in the sanctuary or church. He should adapt carefully the texts and their number to the condition of those who take part in the service. Since in most instances none of the sick will be able to act as reader, the minister should, if possible, invite another person to carry out this office.

Theme: **THE TIME OF SICKNESS IS A TIME OF GRACE**

> **63.** (a) GREETING

> He may greet them in these or similar words:

My dear friends, when Jesus came to preach repentance, he was bringing us good news, for he was proclaiming to us God's love and mercy. Again and again God comes to our help so that we may turn to him and live our lives entirely in his service. Penance is his gift, a gift we should accept with gratitude. Keeping this in mind, let us open our hearts to God with great simplicity and humility and ask to be reconciled with him as we now forgive each other.

If possible, a penitential song is sung by the sick persons, or by a choir.

64. (b) PRAYER

Lord our God,
source of all goodness and mercy,
we come together as your family
to ask your forgiveness
and the forgiveness of each other.
Give us true sorrow for our sins
and loving trust in your compassion
so that we may acknowledge our sins
with sincere hearts.
Through this celebration
restore us to fuller union with yourself
and with our neighbor
so that we may serve you with greater generosity.
We ask this through Christ our Lord.

℟.   Amen.

65. (c) READINGS

The readings may be introduced in these or similar words:

Many people enjoy good health and other blessings and accept them as a matter of course, with no sense of gratitude. In time of sickness we discover that all these are great gifts, and that without them we easily lose heart. God allows us to experience sickness in order to test our faith. What is more, if we see our suffering as a share in Christ's suffering, it can be of great value both to ourselves and to the Church. The time of sickness is not then wasted or meaningless. It is in fact a time of grace if we accept it as God wants us to accept it. This celebration is meant to help us to do so. We shall therefore listen to God's word, examine our conscience, and pray with sincere hearts.

66. FIRST READING Jas 5:13-16

A reading from the Letter of Saint James

Beloved:
Is anyone among you suffering?
He should pray.
Is anyone in good spirits?
He should sing a song of praise.
Is anyone among you sick?
He should summon the presbyters of the Church,
  and they should pray over him
  and anoint him with oil in the name of the Lord.
The prayer of faith will save the sick person,
  and the Lord will raise him up.
If he has committed any sins, he will be forgiven.
Therefore, confess your sins to one another
  and pray for one another, that you may be healed.
The fervent prayer of a righteous person is very powerful.

The word of the Lord.

RESPONSORIAL PSALM

Between the readings, a psalm may be said or sung alternately, for example, Psalm 130 or Psalm 51.

1 Ps 130:1-2, 3-4, 5-6, 7-8

℟. (7bc) With the Lord there is mercy and fullness of redemption.

Out of the depths I cry to you, O LORD;
  LORD, hear my voice!
Let your ears be attentive
  to my voice in supplication.

℟. With the Lord there is mercy and fullness of redemption.

If you, O LORD, mark iniquities,
  LORD, who can stand?
But with you is forgiveness,
  that you may be revered.

℟. With the Lord there is mercy and fullness of redemption.

I trust in the LORD;
  my soul trusts in his word.

More than sentinels wait for the dawn,
  let Israel wait for the LORD.

℟. With the Lord there is mercy and fullness of redemption.

For with the LORD is kindness
  and with him is plenteous redemption;
And he will redeem Israel
  from all their iniquities.

℟. With the Lord there is mercy and fullness of redemption.

2 Ps 51:3-4, 5-6ab, 7-8, 9-11, 12-13, 14 and 17, 19

℟. (see 14a) Give me back the joy of your salvation.

Have mercy on me, O God, in your goodness;
  in the greatness of your compassion wipe out my offense.
Thoroughly wash me from my guilt
  and of my sin cleanse me.

℟. Give me back the joy of your salvation.

For I acknowledge my offense,
  and my sin is before me always:
"Against you only have I sinned,
  and done what is evil in your sight."

℟. Give me back the joy of your salvation.

Indeed, in guilt was I born,
  and in sin my mother conceived me;
Behold, you are pleased with sincerity of heart,
  and in my inmost being you teach me wisdom.

℟. Give me back the joy of your salvation.

Cleanse me of sin with hyssop, that I may be purified;
  wash me, and I shall be whiter than snow.
Let me hear the sounds of joy and gladness;
  the bones you have crushed shall rejoice.
Turn away your face from my sins,
  and blot out all my guilt.

℟. Give me back the joy of your salvation.

A clean heart create for me, O God,
  and a steadfast spirit renew within me.

Cast me not out from your presence,
  and your Holy Spirit take not from me.

℟. Give me back the joy of your salvation.

Give me back the joy of your salvation,
  and a willing spirit sustain in me.
O Lord, open my lips,
  and my mouth shall proclaim your
  praise.

℟. Give me back the joy of your salvation.

My sacrifice, O God, is a contrite spirit;
  a heart contrite and humbled, O God,
  you will not spurn.

℟. Give me back the joy of your salvation.

GOSPEL   Mk 2:1-12

✠ A reading from the holy Gospel
  according to Mark

When Jesus returned to Capernaum after
  some days,
  it became known that he was at home.
Many gathered together so that there was
  no longer room for them,
  not even around the door,
  and he preached the word to them.
They came bringing to him a paralytic carried by four men.
Unable to get near Jesus because of the
  crowd,
  they opened up the roof above him.

After they had broken through,
  they let down the mat on which the paralytic was lying.
When Jesus saw their faith, he said to him,
  "Child, your sins are forgiven."
Now some of the scribes were sitting there
  asking themselves,
  "Why does this man speak that way? He
  is blaspheming.
Who but God alone can forgive sins?"
Jesus immediately knew in his mind what
  they were thinking to themselves,
  so he said, "Why are you thinking such
  things in your hearts?
Which is easier, to say to the paralytic,
  'Your sins are forgiven,'
  or to say, 'Rise, pick up your mat and
  walk'?
But that you may know
  that the Son of Man has authority to forgive sins on earth"
  —he said to the paralytic,
  "I say to you, rise, pick up your mat, and
  go home."
He rose, picked up his mat at once,
  and went away in the sight of everyone.
They were all astounded
  and glorified God, saying, "We have
  never seen anything like this."

The Gospel of the Lord.

67. (d) HOMILY

It is fitting that the celebrant speak of sickness, dwelling not so much on sickness of the body as on sickness of the soul. He should emphasize the power of Jesus and his Church to forgive sins and the value of suffering offered for others.

68. (e) EXAMINATION OF CONSCIENCE

After the homily, the examination of conscience takes place; a sample text is given in Appendix III, page **215**. A period of silence should always be included so that each person may personally examine his conscience.

The following questions may be added but adapted to the condition of the sick:

—Do I trust God's goodness and providence, even in times of stress and illness?

—Do I give in to sickness, to despair, to other unworthy thoughts and feelings?

—Do I fill my empty moments with reflection on life and with prayer to God?

—Do I accept my illness and pain as an opportunity for suffering with Christ, who redeemed us by his passion?

—Do I live by faith, confident that patience in suffering is of great benefit to the Church?

—Am I thoughtful of others and attentive to my fellow patients and their needs?

—Am I grateful to those who look after me and visit me?

—Do I give a good Christian example to others?

—Am I sorry for my past sins, and do I try to make amends for them by my patient acceptance of weakness and illness?

69. (f) ACT OF REPENTANCE

After a moment of silence, all say together:

I confess to almighty God,
and to you, my brothers and sisters,
that I have sinned through my own fault

They strike their breast:

in my thoughts and in my words,
in what I have done,
and in what I have failed to do;
and I ask blessed Mary, ever virgin,
all the angels and saints,
and you, my brothers and sisters,
to pray for me to the Lord our God.

Reader:

Lord our God, we bear the name of your Son and call you Father. We are sorry for our sins against you and against our brothers and sisters.

℟. Give us true repentance and sincere love for you and for our neighbor.

Lord Jesus Christ, you redeemed us by your passion and cross and gave us an example of patience and love. We are sorry for our sins against you, and especially for failing to serve you and our brothers and sisters.

℟. Give us true repentance and sincere love for you and for our neighbor.

Holy Spirit, Lord, you speak to us in the Church and in our conscience and inspire within us the desire to do good. We are sorry for our sins against you, and especially for our obstinate refusal to obey you.

℟. Give us true repentance and sincere love for you and for our neighbor.

Minister:

Let us ask God our Father to forgive us and to free us from evil:

Our Father . . .

70. Then, if possible, the choir or the assembled people sing a song, and the service concludes with a prayer of thanksgiving:

71.

God of consolation and Father of mercies,
you forgive the sinner who acknowledges his guilt:

℟. We praise you and thank you.

God of consolation and Father of mercies,
you give to those who suffer hardship or pain
a share in the sufferings of your Son
for the salvation of the world:

℟. We praise you and thank you.

God of consolation and Father of mercies,
you look with love on those who are troubled or in sorrow;
you give them hope of salvation
and the promise of eternal life:

℟. We praise you and thank you.

Let us pray.

Lord,
your goodness and mercy are boundless.
Look on your sons and daughters
gathered here in the name of your Son.
We thank you for all your gifts
and ask you to keep us always as your family,
full of living faith, firm hope,
and sincere love for you and for our neighbor.
We ask this through Christ our Lord.

℟.   Amen.

72. In place of the prayer, the service may end with a blessing.

May the God of peace
fill your hearts with every blessing.
May he sustain you
with his gifts of hope and consolation,
help you to offer your lives in his service,
and bring you safely to eternal glory.
May almighty God
the Father, and the Son, ✠ and the Holy Spirit,
grant you all that is good.

℟.   Amen.

73. The minister dismisses the assembly, or invites those present to a friendly visit with the sick.

APPENDIX III

FORM OF EXAMINATION OF CONSCIENCE

1. This suggested form for an examination of conscience should be completed and adapted to meet the needs of different individuals and to follow local usages.

2. In an examination of conscience, before the sacrament of penance, each individual should ask himself these questions in particular:

1. What is my attitude to the sacrament of penance? Do I sincerely want to be set free from sin, to turn again to God, to begin a new life, and to enter into a deeper friendship with God? Or do I look on it as a burden, to be undertaken as seldom as possible?

2. Did I forget to mention, or deliberately conceal, any grave sins in past confessions?

3. Did I perform the penance I was given? Did I make reparation for any injury to others? Have I tried to put into practice my resolution to lead a better life in keeping with the Gospel?

3. Each individual should examine his life in the light of God's word.

I. The Lord says: "You shall love the Lord your God with your whole heart."

1. Is my heart set on God, so that I really love him above all things and am faithful to his commandments, as a son loves his father? Or am I more concerned about the things of this world? Have I a right intention in what I do?

2. God spoke to us in his Son. Is my faith in God firm and secure? Am I wholehearted in accepting the Church's teaching? Have I been careful to grow in my understanding of the faith, to hear God's word, to listen to instructions on the faith, to avoid dangers to faith? Have I been always strong and fearless in professing my faith in God and the Church? Have I been willing to be known as a Christian in private and public life?

3. Have I prayed morning and evening? When I pray, do I really raise my mind and heart to God or is it a matter of words only? Do I offer God my difficulties, my joys, and my sorrows? Do I turn to God in time of temptation?

4. Have I love and reverence for God's name? Have I offended him in blasphemy, swearing falsely, or taking his name in vain? Have I shown disrespect for the Blessed Virgin Mary and the saints?

5. Do I keep Sundays and feast days holy by taking a full part, with attention and devotion, in the liturgy, and especially in the Mass? Have I fulfilled the precept of annual confession and of communion during the Easter season?

6. Are there false gods that I worship by giving them greater attention and deeper trust than I give to God: money, superstition, spiritism, or other occult practices?

II.   The Lord says: "Love one another as I have loved you."

1. Have I a genuine love for my neighbors? Or do I use them for my own ends, or do to them what I would not want done to myself? Have I given grave scandal by my words or actions?

2. In my family life, have I contributed to the well-being and happiness of the rest of the family by patience and genuine love? Have I been obedient to parents, showing them proper respect and giving them help in their spiritual and material needs? Have I been careful to give a Christian upbringing to my children, and to help them by good example and by exercising authority as a parent. Have I been faithful to my husband (wife) in my heart and in my relations with others?

3. Do I share my possessions with the less fortunate? Do I do my best to help the victims of oppression, misfortune, and poverty? Or do I look down on my neighbor, especially the poor, the sick, the elderly, strangers, and people of other races?

4. Does my life reflect the mission I received in confirmation? Do I share in the apostolic and charitable works of the Church and in the life of my parish? Have I helped to meet the needs of the Church and of the world and prayed for them: for unity in the Church, for the spread of the Gospel among the nations, for peace and justice, etc.?

5. Am I concerned for the good and prosperity of the human community in which I live, or do I spend my life caring only for myself? Do I share to the best of my ability in the work of promoting justice, morality, harmony, and love in human relations? Have I done my duty as a citizen? Have I paid my taxes?

6. In my work or profession am I just, hard-working, honest, serving society out of love for others? Have I paid a fair wage to my employees? Have I been faithful to my promises and contracts?

7. Have I obeyed legitimate authority and given it due respect?

8. If I am in a position of responsibility or authority, do I use this for my own advantage or for the good of others, in a spirit of service?

9. Have I been truthful and fair, or have I injured others by deceit, calumny, detraction, rash judgment, or violation of a secret?

10. Have I done violence to others by damage to life or limb, reputation, honor, or material possessions? Have I involved them in loss? Have I been responsible for advising an abortion or procuring one? Have I kept up hatred for others? Am I estranged from others through quarrels, enmity, insults, anger? Have I been guilty of refusing to testify to the innocence of another because of selfishness?

11. Have I stolen the property of others? Have I desired it unjustly and inordinately? Have I damaged it? Have I made restitution of other people's property and made good their loss?

12. If I have been injured, have I been ready to make peace for the love of Christ and to forgive, or do I harbor hatred and the desire for revenge?

III. Christ our Lord says: "Be perfect as your Father is perfect."

1. Where is my life really leading me? Is the hope of eternal life my inspiration? Have I tried to grow in the life of the Spirit through prayer, reading the word of God and meditating on it, receiving the sacraments, self-denial? Have I been anxious to control my vices, my bad inclinations and passions, e.g., envy, love of food and drink? Have I been proud and boastful, thinking myself better in the sight of God and despising others as less important than myself? Have I imposed my own will on others, without respecting their freedom and rights?

2. What use have I made of time, of health and strength, of the gifts God has given me to be used like the talents in the Gospel? Do I use them to become more perfect every day? Or have I been lazy and too much given to leisure?

3. Have I been patient in accepting the sorrows and disappointments of life? How have I performed mortification so as to "fill up what is

wanting to the sufferings of Christ"? Have I kept the precept of fasting and abstinence?

4. Have I kept my senses and my whole body pure and chaste as a temple of the Holy Spirit consecrated for resurrection and glory, and as a sign of God's faithful love for men and women, a sign that is seen most perfectly in the sacrament of matrimony? Have I dishonored my body by fornication, impurity, unworthy conversation or thoughts, evil desires, or actions? Have I given in to sensuality? Have I indulged in reading, conversation, shows, and entertainments that offend against Christian and human decency? Have I encouraged others to sin by my own failure to maintain these standards? Have I been faithful to the moral law in my married life?

5. Have I gone against my conscience out of fear or hypocrisy?

6. Have I always tried to act in the true freedom of the sons of God according to the law of the Spirit or am I the slave of forces within me?